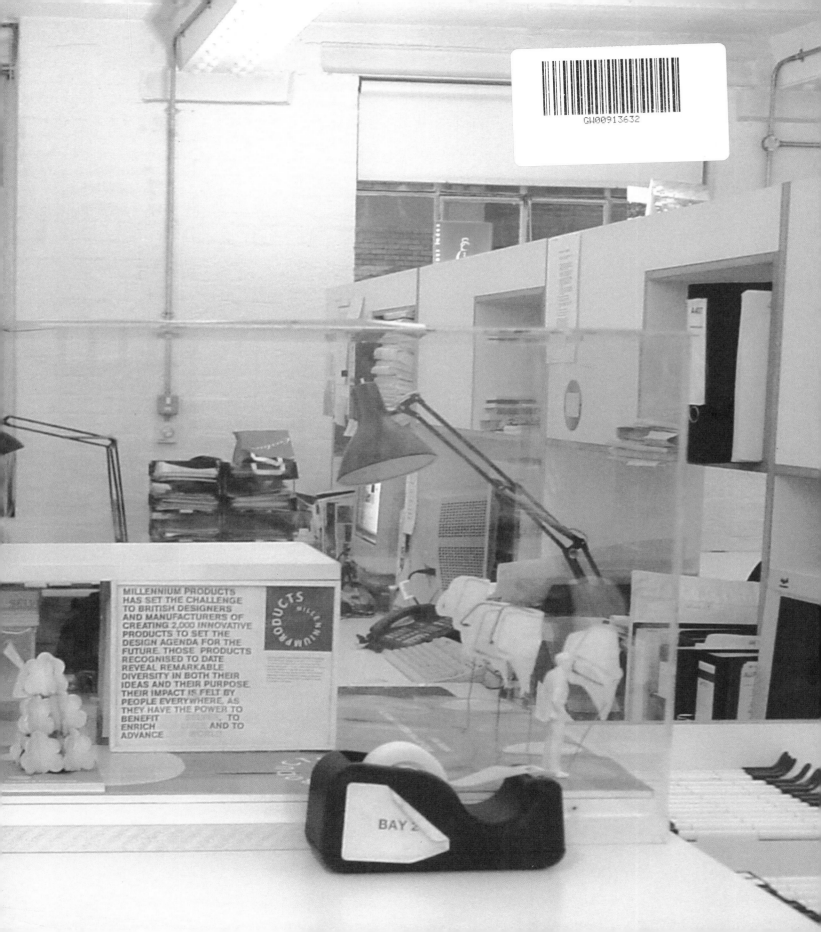

MILLENNIUM PRODUCTS HAS SET THE CHALLENGE TO BRITISH DESIGNERS AND MANUFACTURERS OF CREATING 2,000 INNOVATIVE PRODUCTS TO SET THE DESIGN AGENDA FOR THE FUTURE. THOSE PRODUCTS RECOGNISED TO DATE REVEAL REMARKABLE DIVERSITY IN BOTH THEIR IDEAS AND THEIR PURPOSE. THEIR IMPACT IS FELT BY PEOPLE EVERYWHERE, AS THEY HAVE THE POWER TO BENEFIT   , TO ENRICH   AND TO ADVANCE

MILLENNIUMPRODUCTS

BAY 2

Manual

the architecture and office of Allford Hall Monaghan Morris

Iain Borden

Birkhäuser – Publishers for Architecture
Basel • Boston • Berlin

A CIP catalogue record for this book is available from
the Library of Congress, Washington D.C., USA.

Bibliographic information published
by Die Deutsche Bibliothek
Die Deutsche Bibliothek lists this publication in the
Deutsche Nationalbibliografie; detailed bibliographic
data is available in the Internet at <http://dnb.ddb.de>.

© 2003 Birkhäuser – Publishers for Architecture,
P.O. Box 133, CH-4010 Basel, Switzerland.
Member of the BertelsmannSpringer
Publishing Group.

Text © 2003 the authors.
The moral right of the authors has been asserted

All plans and drawings © the architects.
Photography: see credits on page 239

Printed on acid-free paper produced of
chlorine-free pulp. TCF ∞
Printed in Germany
ISBN 3-7643-6755-5

9 8 7 6 5 4 3 2 1
http://www.birkhauser.ch

Design: Studio Myerscough

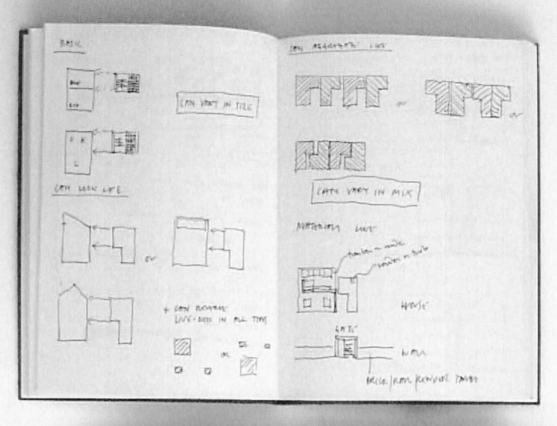

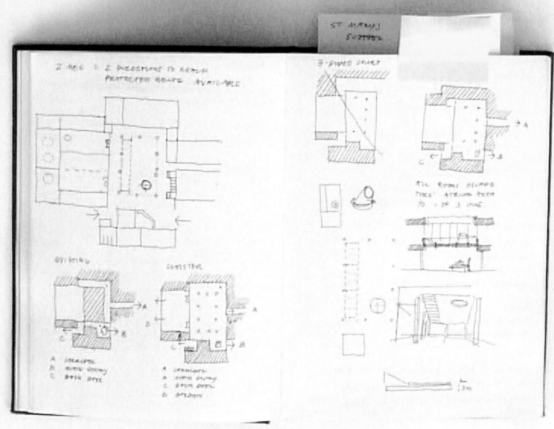

ALLFORD HALL MONAGHAN MORRIS

Allford Hall Monaghan Morris
Architects
2nd Floor, Block B
Morelands
5 - 23 Old Street
London EC1V 9HL

T 0207 251 5261
F 0207 251 5123
E info@ahmm.co.uk

Project

Subject

Job No.   File Ref

Date

Sheet   of

By

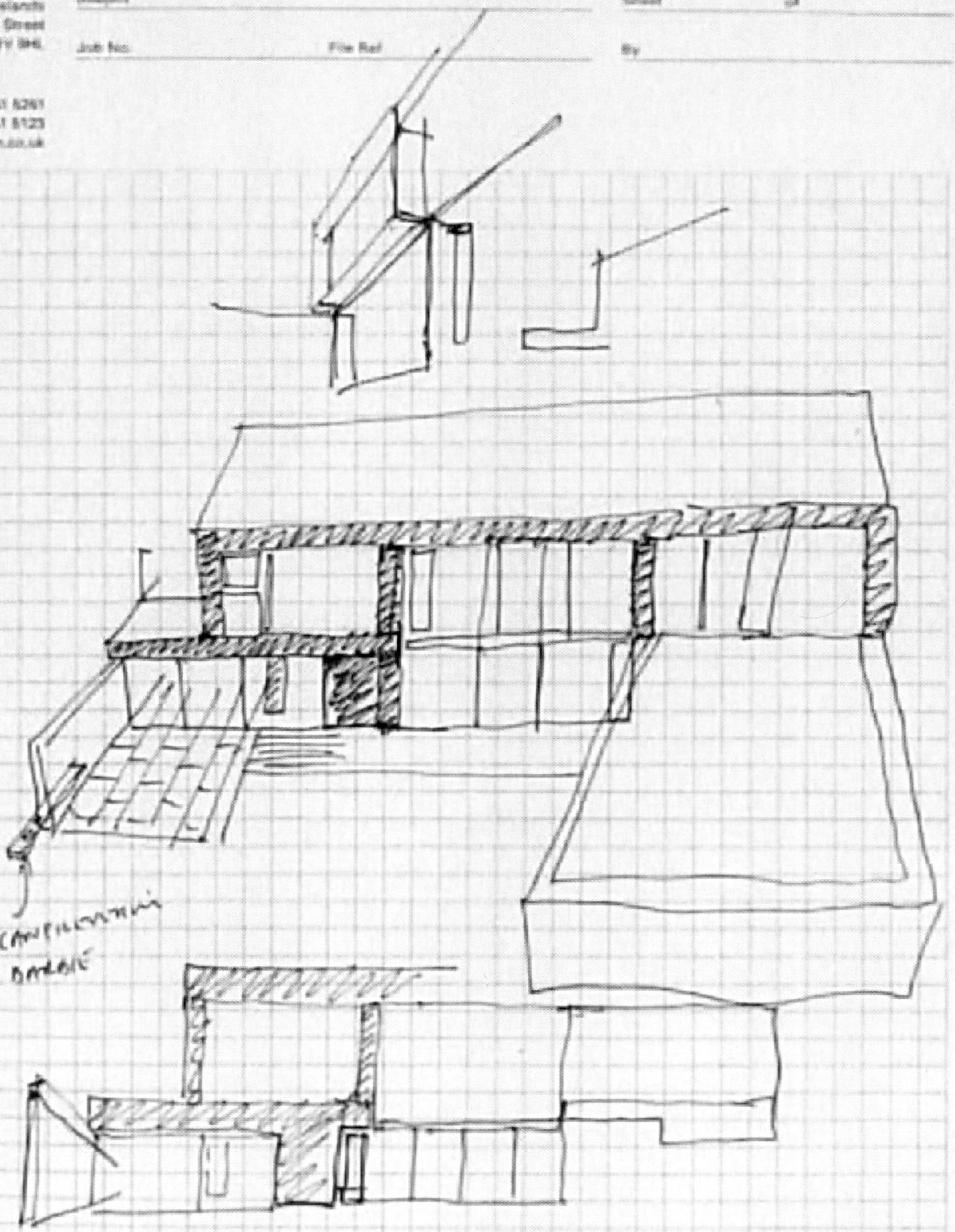

CAMPILLICANTHON
BARLOIS

Preface

I had known Simon Allford, Jonathan Hall, Paul Monaghan and Peter Morris as friends long before this book began. Early bar conversations about maybe doing some kind of book about something to do with architecture sometime in the future finally turned serious in late-1999. Quite what this book would be was still unclear: not solely a monograph, for sure, but a book also about architecture, architectural practice and their own office and design; about AHMM, but not a chronological project-by-project account; focused on ideas, but always architectural and not over-laden with critical theory; something serious, but which also explored the accidental, changeable and downright you'd-cry-if-you-didn't-laugh nature of architectural practice.

We entered into a protracted two-year period of interviews (first between myself and each of the four partners, and then collectively between all five), visits to buildings, image reviews and innumerable continuing conversations about what the book might be. Somewhere in the middle of all this emerged a structure of thematic sections contained within a manual-like approach to explanation and interpretation. Another year or so of writing and editing, and a close involvement with designers Studio Myerscough, editor Nick Barley and publishers Birkhäuser, and Manual has finally arrived.

Like all of AHMM's work, this book is the result of a process involving gestation, collaboration, and a willingness to let the final product mutate according to constraints, opportunities and developing thoughts. It has evolved rather than been pre-determined. And it is finished as a published book, but incomplete as a continuing conversation.

Iain Borden
London 2003

Acknowledgements

A great number of people have offered thoughts, opinions and suggestions during the gestation of Manual – far too many to thank individually here. So a collective thanks to everyone for all those snippets of information and odd stories, gentle prods and subtle warnings, raised eyebrows and wry smiles, why-don't-you's and how-about's.

I must acknowledge the special contributions of Nick Barley at August and of Morag Myerscough and David Lowbridge at Studio Myerscough for their immense efforts and creative expertise in helping to develop, refine and finally produce this book. Similarly, I have been in no small way dependent on the contribution of the AHMM office, who provided information and help, as well as the vast majority of the images reproduced here – particular thanks are due here to Matt Chisnall. I am also indebted to the contributors, who graciously took time and trouble to write the accompanying essays and texts, some at short notice. Thanks are also due to Jane Rendell, who provided her usual conceptual sounding board. Claire Haywood provided encouragement and support, and more than once had to explain to me some of the finer details of real architectural practice.

And, of course, I am wholly indebted to Simon, Jonathan, Paul and Peter, first for inviting me to work on this project, and then for opening up their office, archives and ideas in such a frank and open-minded manner – their readiness to do something different, to follow through, and to commit, is truly exceptional.

Of all the time spent working on Manual, the most delightful was a wonderful day in Wiltshire, at the Poolhouse, in the company of Beryl Allford. This book is dedicated to her and to David Allford.

Introduction

A manual, typically, tells you what is what. It sets out the key components of an object or problem, identifying them in a logical manner. It delineates how to engage with those components, letting you know what to do, when to do it, and with what consequences. A manual assumes a simple, direct relationship between you (the operator) and the object (the field of operation), and from that assumption a coded and complete knowledge is erected. A manual instils confidence and competence. It is a book of instructions.

This manual is not quite like that. Nor indeed, should any such guide to architecture ever be quite like that, for, unlike instrumentalist relations of knowledge and object, the equivalent connection between knowledge and architecture is necessarily more complicated.

Most obviously, there is the most direct form of architectural knowledge, the knowledge that we might need in order to practice architecture. How do we know what to design and construct? What are the appropriate forms, structures, services, spaces, technologies to incorporate into an architectural project, and how do we come to decide upon them?

In addition, the practising of architecture itself is a unique kind of knowledge. Between the absolute judgments of science or the purely poetic speculations of art, architecture offers an iterative, dialogic way of knowing the world, which is at once purposeful yet uncertain, utopic yet pragmatic, interventionist yet reactive. In deciding what to design and to construct, one must be aware that the solution can never be pre-formed, pre-determined or previously understood. The knowledge produced though the practising of architecture is provisional.

Furthermore, in practising architecture it could be said that we come to know the world in a different kind of way. Architecture is a critical practice by which one is continually reflecting on the problems at hand, the solutions on offer, the ways of working and proceeding which might be taken and, ultimately, upon the kinds of social engagements that this architecture might produce, between people and the world around them, people and objects, people and other people. Architecture is coded but never comprehensive. It is ambitious, but never complete.

The particular manual which now rests in your hands is not a guide as to what to do when practising architecture. Well, it is, but not in the way which you might immediately think. There are no final prescriptions or proscriptions here, no one-liner philosophies of overly serious intent. There is no singular truth on offer here, no finality, no ends, no absolutes. There are, however, lots of different kinds of truths, lots of starting points, pathways, tendencies and contingent relations. This is a work of maxims, of rules of thumb and of proven and yet-to-be-proven adages; it encompasses architectural ideas derived from insight, inspiration and sweated creativity; and it contains operations derived from critical practice of all kinds: testings, experiments, prototyping and uncertain effects.

Above all, this is a manual of architecture as it has been and is being undertaken by Allford Hall Monaghan Morris, the architectural practice formed in London by Simon Allford, Jonathan Hall, Paul Monaghan and Peter Morris. AHMM (as the practice is often referred to) is continually extending an extraordinary range of constructions – from medical practices, offices and social housing to transport interchanges, poolhouses and lofts, to ephemeral art collaborations, exhibition pavilions and theoretical propositions. By exploiting the diversity of this portfolio the office is enacting a multi-faceted yet co-ordinated form of architectural endeavour, one which is concerned not only with architecture as object and design but also as a way of engaging with the city and landscape, responding to clients and users, collaborating with engineers and artists, and indeed as a way of engaging with how architecture itself is done. Hence the sub-title of this book, addressing both architecture as a discipline and AHMM as an office, as a process of creating architecture. Manual is about the work of an architectural practice getting out there and doing it, of producing architecture as substance, thought and operation.

As a consequence, we hope that this book marks a small shift in the way in which architecture is currently being published and discussed. Anyone browsing the architectural shelves of a bookshop cannot help but notice that the vast majority of publications focus not only on the work of architectural designers but also, even more directly, on the way that their buildings look, i.e. on the forms, shapes and spaces of a kind of architecture which is comprehended predominantly as a visual entity. By comparison, those publications which seek to discuss architectural design other than as a purely visual entity are relatively thin on the ground. Manual seeks to rectify this situation by looking at architecture as a practice and as an office, as a process which involves not only form and visuality but also spatial dispositions, frameworks and technologies, as actions, collaborations and opportunities, as elements, materials and plans, as accidents, chances and surprises, as money and luck both good and bad. Manual is therefore not so much a manual as to how architecture might look, but as to how it might also be practised, how it might proceed, how it might operate. It is, in short, a manual to all that might be architecture as created in the work of Allford Hall Monaghan Morris.

1:0   Non-style

In the last hundred years or so all things have become increasingly judged on the way they look. We tend to value food, cars and clothes as well as lovers, friends and colleagues according to a contrast of colour, the twist of a curve, the cut of a suit, the line of a fringe; in this scopic world, shapes, colours, forms and style are the obsessed qualities of desire. Architecture, very often, is treated no differently. As ebullient shapes and disjunctive forms, architecture is often expected to demonstrate a visual wow-factor that dominates over all else, an impact-on-the-eye that stops architectural spectators dead in their tracks. Moreover, in a further reduction of architecture to the realm of the visual, architects can even sometimes consider the photographic effect of a building to be more important than the way it looks in 'real life'; as H.S. Goodhart-Rendel once remarked, the building is merely the necessary inconvenience which has to take place between the initial drawing and the final photograph. Such a focus on the visual is not purely due to the ideas of designers; critics and historians of architecture also too often focus on what architecture 'looks like' (a wireless, a carbuncle, a chemical refinery?) rather than on what it does, represents or means, or on how it operates, stands up or has been conceived.

Architecture is, of course, about far more than appearances, and this has major ramifications for an understanding of architectural practice as design process. It is here, then, that we begin to identify design as a wider process, as a means, perhaps, of inquiry or discovery, of procedure or process, of relations and connections – anything, that is, other than a fixed, a priori notion of appearance, looks or style. This does not mean that the architecture which results from such a process has no concern with the visual – far from it. Rather that the visual is allowed to be encultured and enriched as the project develops through its complex stages. The visual, as with all aspects of architectural design, becomes a journey of discovery.

What is important, therefore, is to allow that journey to take place, giving the architecture time in which to evolve, and encouraging qualities other than the purely visual to emerge. Indeed, as Cedric Price has noted, good design is often a matter of delaying the making of decisions so that, at different moments and at different places, timely and pertinent questions might get asked.

Project 1:1 North Croydon Medical Centre	**> Context and comment** > Surgery for the busy practice of a GP. > The client approached the office after viewing the AHMM-curated 'Designing for Doctors' exhibition.
Date 1995–99	> An extended planning process involved four re-designs covering three schemes (mono-pitch, flat roof and the final pitched-roof options). Planners focused entirely on an adjoining Edwardian building, while ignoring the modernist 1960s hospital on the opposite side. The planners even decided to draw and fax over their own designs – which were rejected by the architects.
Location Croydon	
Client Dr Robert J Trew	> Cellular rooms for private consultations and offices are positioned within a sheltering pitched roof element held against the site edge, while the intermediary slot space connecting to the street terrace is more lightweight in construction, and contains reception, entrance, circulation and an enclosed courtyard. A brick base provides anti-vandal, street-corner toughness, while higher elevations play formal games with the fenestration. > The building is promoted in an official government design guide for medical centres and for 'good design' in general.

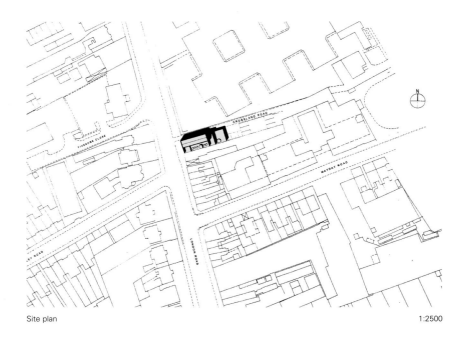

Site plan   1:2500

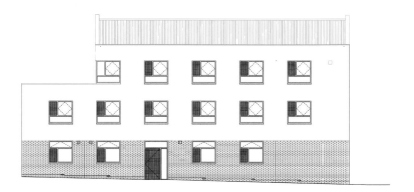

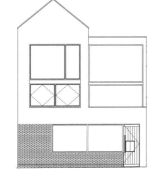

North Elevation   West Elevation   1:250

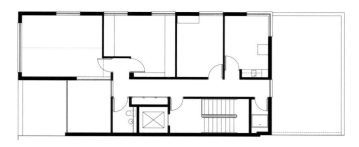

Second floor plan

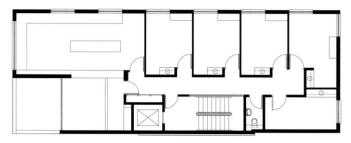

First floor plan

Ground floor plan

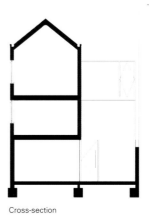

Cross-section

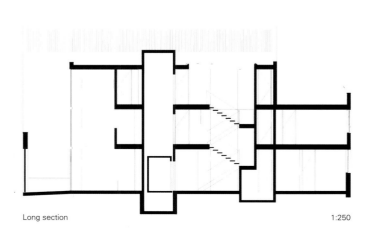

Long section

1:250

1:1.1 Disposition

It is not necessary for a building design to be a complete architecture at an early stage of the development process. What is crucial is to get the overall disposition right, and then to develop an architecture within that guiding strategy. With North Croydon Medical Centre, that strategy is evident in the general spatial arrangement of volumes and in composition of plan. This allows, among other things, the pull-back of the slot space and open courtyard, thus creating a sequence of transitional, intermediary and calming zones between the exposed grittiness of the external street and the professional intimacy of the medical consultation – a hierarchy of space which becomes increasingly private as you get further inside and higher up the building.

1:1.2 Differential rules

Working from inside out, three differently composed elevations are extruded onto the exterior. On the long, left-hand elevation a neatly patterned articulation of the window groupings reveals the cellular spaces behind. At the rear, a more private and less formal arrangement includes a structure-denying corner aperture punched into the upper right of the building.

More complex is the public front elevation, where comparisons with Mondrian and De Stijl are inevitable through its forceful deployment of geometry and colour. Balanced against these conceptual correlations are some more pragmatic concerns for each window simply to do what it has to do: the ground-level glazings (screening the waiting room) are etched for privacy, on the first floor the square panels open on to the offices, while the single vertical yellow panel is sized for the ventilation into the staff room above.

Although apparently highly rational in its ordering, there is a quirkiness to the elevation in the way in which the right-hand structure of the office element of the building, in the centre of the composition, does not come down right through the lowest window as one might expect, but instead is brought to terminate on a massive horizontal beam. Similarly, the left mullion of the lowest, etched window does not line up with the office windows above but is determined by the waiting room space which it serves. A comparison with another AHMM building known as Portsmouth Players, where windows in the brick walls are indeed made to align, is telling; at the Medical Centre the lower window is set within a different material (brick) to the office structure above (white rendered concrete), so alternative conceptual and compositional rules can indeed apply.

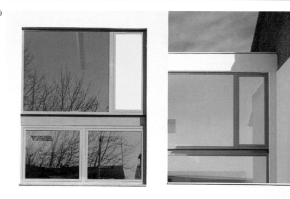

Fig 6 Triple-height
void over the
reception area

Fig 7 Evening view of
north-west corner

Fig 8 East elevation

Fig 9 West elevation
detail

Fig 10 Doctor's
consulting room

Fig 11 Void over
reception area

Overleaf:
West elevation

1:1.3 Composition

Similar compositions are also generated internally as the design develops. Within a private consulting room, the glazed windows are displaced right into the corner. To generate an overall square fenestration element, while ceding to fire requirements for a limit on the overall area of glass, a solid yellow panel is added. To the right, a bookshelf acts as a positive mirrored reflection of the lowermost window element.

1:1.4 Void + void

The gradual evolution of the spatial strategy enables the luxury and drama of a doubled triple-height void to be established. One void hovers over the roofless internal courtyard, conceptually contained by the overall footprint of the building. The second sits over the reception space, and is enclosed within the building envelope.

The true significance of AHMM: Notorious marketeers who had a brand before they had any buildings. But in this age where English architecture amounts to the commercials claiming quality design and our great designers embracing commercialism, AHMM represent a third way.

They use all means to get a foot in the door. Once through, however, they ignore their own propaganda and get down to the hard graft of good design. Pretensions seldom evaporate amongst the new elite and they make a refreshing change – curiously old-fashioned like BDP or YRM used to be; enjoying life but utterly focused on the quality of their work.

Matthew Wells

Project 1:2	> Context and comment
CASPAR	> Scheme won in competition.

Date
1999–2000

Location
Birmingham

Client
Joseph Rowntree
Foundation

> Over 4.3 million new households will be formed in the UK by 2020 – many being single people looking to rent living accommodation at an affordable cost. This market sector is largely ignored by a construction industry which tends to focus on expensive out-of-town homes and inner city two-bed apartments.

> This low-cost rental sector is targeted by the CASPAR (City-centre Apartments for Single People at Affordable Rents) housing initiative, set up by the Joseph Rowntree Foundation.

> The Birmingham CASPAR, located in an inner city industrial quarter, posits a unique prototype for urban living: two blocks eight metres apart conceived as individual structures with four elevations, connected by end-glazing, an over-sailing roof and a courtyard. Exteriors are steel frames and red brick, the inner courtyard is clad in opepe hardwood, while private bridges (not shared decks) provide access to individual one-bedroom apartments.

> There is absolutely no fat here, the entire project being constructed for under £52,000 per unit, inclusive of all fittings and fees.

> Prefabricated bathroom modules and a variety of other research-intensive specification decisions all help to limit costs.

> Residents enjoy highly competitive rents combined with easy access to New Street train station, the Birmingham Rep and Symphony Hall, the nightlife of Broad St and a Ronnie Scott's jazz club.

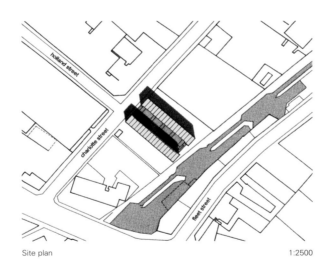

Site plan   1:2500

Cross section   1:400

Typical upper floor plan

First floor plan

Long section

1:400

Fig 1 Exterior apartment
balconies

Fig 2 View of
Holland Street
from an
apartment

Fig 3 Canal-side
context

1:2.1 Profit and prototype
When innovatively linked and developed, economic
advantage and architectural design can become
symbiotic beneficiaries.

Through the design for CASPAR, Rowntree wish to
demonstrate that not only high-cost, high-end housing
can be economically profitable. CASPAR thus sets out
to show how low-cost apartments can be built as an
investment, sold on to long-term speculators such
as pension and insurance funds, and rented out at
reasonable sums while still giving good income return.
Investors can expect a good 6–7% return, and initial
assessments indicate that it could be as much as 9%.

Architecturally, the challenges of the low-cost rental
sector have led to the formulation of a new generic
prototype, where circulation is simultaneously
minimised and celebrated as the apartment dweller's
own route to their individual home. Quite distinct
from older urban types such as the mansion flat,
deck access block or perimeter courtyard block, the
Birmingham CASPAR is also flexible enough to be
readily modified for larger apartments with two
or more bedrooms, or to be refined through the
development of particular design elements such
as bigger bridges or balconies.

1:2.2 Diversities
CASPAR's residents are neither homogeneous in
nature nor restricted by its architecture. Tenants
range from 20- and 30-something urban professionals
seeking immediate access to the delights of the
city, to older 'empty nesters' undertaking a newly
independent life after divorce or bereavement. In all
cases, CASPAR encourages residents' connectivity
with the city through location and view, the block being
set at right angles to the canal in order to provide all
apartments with views of water and city. The same
applies to the temporality of the scheme, for these are
'lifetime homes', fully accessible and usable by those
with physical disabilities. Some may well choose to
stay for just a few months while others can stay on
for as long as they wish.

1:2.3 Social condenser
The angled flying bridges provide defensible space as
private entrance, front garden and bicycle storage
for individual residents. But these are not entirely
private territories – together with the interconnecting
longitudinal bridges they act as places where people
can see and meet each other, alternatively displaying,
greeting, conversing or safely avoiding as mood and
moment might suggest.

Other aspects of CASPAR's design reinforce this
theatrical atmosphere. The gently sloping ground floor
gives a sense of arrival into the courtyard, while the
glazed block ends and open-sided roof impart a feeling
of spatial generosity and peaceful light that is often
missing from the more conventional courtyard format.
The double-aspect of each living room, with views out
into both the city/canal and the courtyard, provides
discreet social connectivity. Taken together, these
bridges, courtyard and views allow CASPAR to operate
as a kind of giant social condenser – a zone where
people both live separately and come together, doing
so in manner that avoids the sharp and artificial
demarcation between the public and the private, the
inside and the out, the familiar and the unfamiliar.

4

5

Fig 4 Apartment
living room

Fig 5 Competition
model

Fig 6 Apartment
living room

Fig 7 View into
internal courtyard

Fig 8 Internal courtyard
elevation

Fig 9 View from
Holland Street

Overleaf:
CASPAR, internal
courtyard with shared
walkways and private,
flying bridge entrances

6

7

8

9

Quoted from David Dunster,
'Caspar 1: Allford Hall Monaghan
Morris in Birmingham',
Architecture Today , 107,
(April 2000), pp. 22-8.

Prototype

During the past 25 years, housing has floundered in the undergrowth of architectural discourse. Lacking both political drive and architectural moralism, housing for the masses dropped out of mainstream practice and teaching. But now a radical change is afoot, marked not least by Allford Hall Monaghan Morris's new scheme in Birmingham for the Joseph Rowntree Foundation, which ironically began life doing the same work in Victorian times. Without any doubt it is a splendid building and the differences between it and the predecessors of the 50s and 60s merit discussion. Unlike those earlier works, the funding process exhibits significant changes which open up cheaper housing provision in cities to a combination of private finance and public initiative. As an explicit experiment, the lessons that I can draw from it indicate that it should be treated as a prototype and not as a one-off exercise. [...]

The building sits on the site with elegance and adds to the matrix of buildings that makes up the Jewellery Quarter. Rowntree have good architects here, who won the competition with a prototype of future urban rental accommodation. Prototypes need to be monitored in use and in terms of running costs. As Emilio Ambasz argued in the 70s, prototypes derive from archetypes and can give birth to stereotypes. If the archetype is the urban barn (the forerunners could be any historic cathedral or Inigo Jones church, the great market buildings of Padua and Vicenza, and railway stations) then this is the first time the barn has become urban housing. There are variations on the plans, elevations, services and structure to be explored. This building is good enough to not be a one-off.

David Dunster

Project 1:3	> **Context and comment**
Live-In Room House	> Design for an exhibition on the 'House for the Future'.

Date
1994

> Constructed almost entirely of different kinds of glass – clear and opaque, structural and non-structural, heat-emitting and sun-reflecting.

Location
The Architecture
Foundation, London

> An experimental socio-spatial agenda redefines the nature of the house and its relationship to its inhabitants and surrounding landscape.

> To effectively explore the project, a battery of communicative media techniques are deployed, ranging from precise models and explanatory diagrams to video animation and cartoon-derived drawings. Refer to *Surface/Live-In Room House*.

Client
N/A

> Conceived initially as a purely theoretical exhibition project, Live-In Room House later came close to being constructed on the remote Scottish island of Skye.

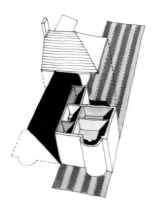

Typical suburban plot

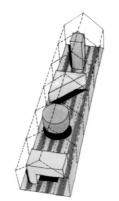

Live-In Room House

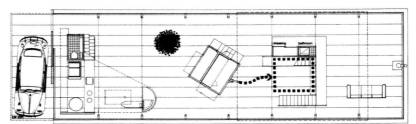

Plan

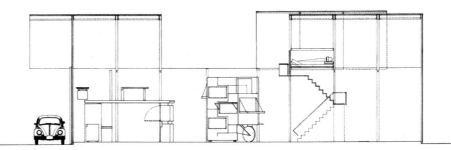

Long section

Section through kitchen

Section through court   1:200

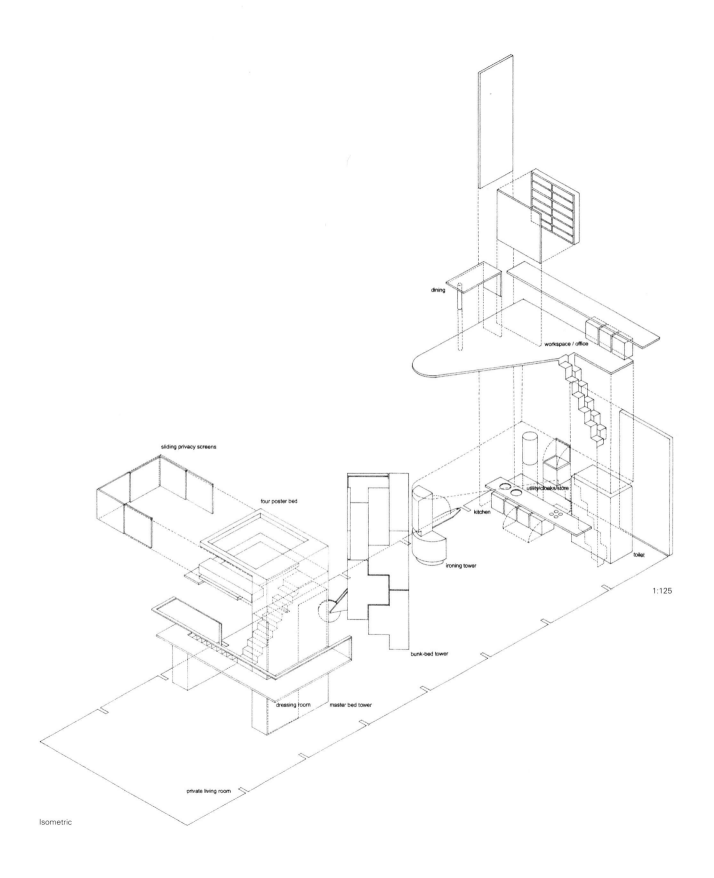

dining

workspace / office

sliding privacy screens

four poster bed

utility/cloaks/store

kitchen

ironing tower

toilet

bunk-bed tower

dressing room   master bed tower

private living room

Isometric

1:125

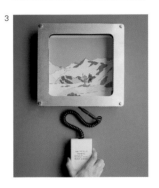

1:3.1 Expanded field

The most common type of suburban house plot places the house at the front and the garden, taking up the remainder of the site, at the rear. Live-In Room House rejects that normative spatial configuration, not by subtle rearrangement but by negating the whole logic of a distinct separation of house and garden as discrete elements.

The garden is brought within the expanded perimeter of the house, which now occupies the entire plot. All kinds of room – whether bathroom, bedroom, kitchen, study, or wine cellar – are erased and reconceptualised as brightly coloured 'functional mechanisms' which are then placed like furniture within the total volume.

The overall consequence is a reconfiguration of domestic space – neither inside nor out, but decentred into the expanded field of the available land.

1:3.2 Research and experimentation

Central to the appearance of the Live-In Room House is its exploitation of newly available, advanced technological kinds of glass, made possible by the close involvement of structural engineer Tim Macfarlane of Dewhurst Macfarlane. Beside such things as heat-emitting, furniture-specific and structural glass, the project also contains an early use of Privalite, made by Saint Gobain – a glass laminate with a liquid crystal interlayer. When a low electric current is passed through Privalite, the crystals are aligned and the glass sandwich becomes transparent. Conversely, turning the electricity off makes the crystals relax and the glass becomes opaque. What you see is not necessarily what you get.

When combined with Aerogel clear insulation to provide appropriate U-values, the potential application to a domestic project becomes immediately evident: a house which has no need of permanent opacity and which is unconstrained by conventional rules about glass and heat conservation.

Fig 1 Model detail showing 'functional mechanism'

Fig 2 Live-In Room House model

Fig 3 Opaque Privalite (current off)

Fig 4 Transparent Privalite (current on)

Fig 5 Wall section with Privalite and Aerogel

Fig 6 Isle of Skye project

Fig 7 Animated computer model created by Mark Logue

Opposite: The model

1:3.3 Coloured space

The house is almost completely transparent, the full length of the internal volume being discernible both to external observers and internal users due to the near total use of glass. Vision and movement around the house, it is suggested, are equally fluid and without barrier.

Yet this very transparency is constantly variegated and occasionally denied by the use of colour for different spatial and furniture modules. These colour-defined elements in turn alter the perceived materiality of the internal space; space itself becomes alternatively intensified or knocked back, refracted or reflected, present or absent, obstructive or permeable. Overall, space is not clear or transparent, homogeneous or static, but modulated and coloured.

'In order to raise culture to a higher level, we are forced, whether we like it or not, to change our architecture. And this will be possible only if we free the rooms in which we live of their enclosed character. This, however, we can do only by introducing a glass architecture which admits the light of the sun, moon and stars into the rooms, not only through windows but through as many walls as possible, these to consist entirely of glass – of coloured glass.'

Paul Scheerbart, *Glasarchitektur* (1914).

1:3.4 Non-canon

According to the conventional history of architectural modernism, any house made of glass must have a flat roof. Canonic predecessors such as the Farnsworth House (Mies van der Rohe) and the Glass House at New Canaan (Philip Johnson) more or less dictate as much. Live-In Room House avoids this kind of categorisation, boasting a resolutely pitched roof which not only negates the rules set up by Mies and Johnson, but whose forthright angle is calculated to conjure up associations with a child's playhouse. Live-In Room House is architectural modernism of an idiomatic but not enslaved breed.

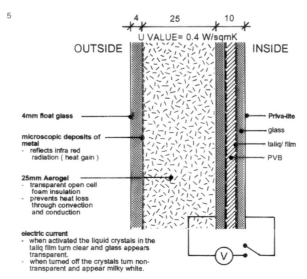

Wall section with Privalite and Aerogel

$$U \text{ VALUE} = 0.4 \text{ W/sqmK}$$

4   25   10

OUTSIDE   INSIDE

4mm float glass

microscopic deposits of metal
- reflects infra red radiation (heat gain)

25mm Aerogel
- transparent open cell foam insulation
- prevents heat loss through convection and conduction

electric current
- when activated the liquid crystals in the taliq film turn clear and glass appears transparent.
- when turned off the crystals turn non-transparent and appear milky white.

Priva-lite
glass
taliq/ film
PVB

V

Project 1:4
Portsmouth Players

Date
1999

Location
Portsmouth

Client
Portsmouth Players

> **Context and comment**
> Refurbishment and extension of the home of an amateur dramatics company by updating the historic thatched barn housing the troupe's rehearsal space and rationalising their outhouses into a new, adjoining two-storey structure.

> A simple box deforms and articulates itself in order to accommodate the programme and connection to the existing barn. The general mood is of a tough but carefully wrought casket placed within a green park setting.

> Portsmouth Players is intensively inhabited while also completed within a tight budget: £215,000 for both the new structure and the refurbished barn.

> An architecture that is understated not only in the quiet presence of the building but also in the architect's own refusal to grab the starring role.

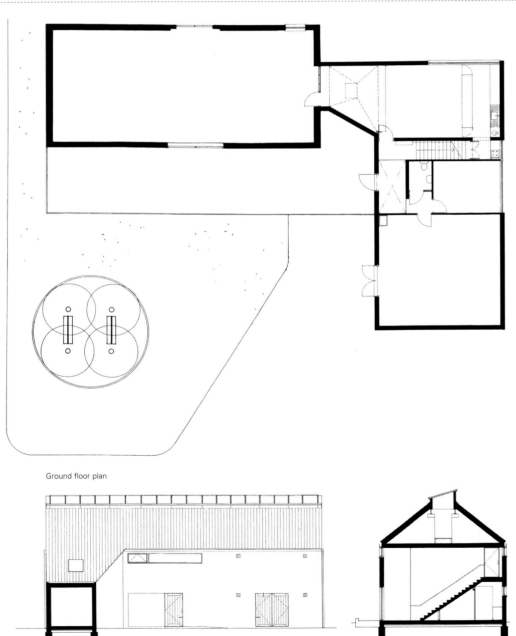

Ground floor plan

West elevation

Section through entrance   1:250

Fig 1 North elevation

Fig 2 Fundraising party
in the park

Fig 3 Poster for a
production at
Portsmouth Players

Fig 4 View from
north-east

Fig 5 Rehearsal
space

Fig 6 Section
through link

Fig 7 East elevation

Overleaf:
West elevation

1:4.1 Linkage

A common English architectural scenario: how to link a new building to an existing structure possessed of a definite historical character. A deformed new building extrudes downward and clips directly onto the old barn. The quirkiness of this unusual act is heightened by a tension between the symmetry of one end and the asymmetry of the other. Deliberately different to the conventional modernist 'new + link + old' three-box solution, the isolationist air of a pavilion-in-the-park is replaced by a more adaptive yet equally forthright kind of architecture.

1:4.2 Mannered reaction

The threat of vandalism dictates the use of minimally-sized external windows, whose very smallness increases their apparent disruption to what are otherwise largely blank brick-faced elevations. Playing with this condition, the internal plan is allowed to force somewhat surprising window dispositions. On the north side, for example, the lower ribbon window is pushed to the extreme left of the wall, while the right edge of this linear element neatly aligns with the equivalent right edge of a higher, this time centrally placed square window. The opposite of the ad hoc approach to architectural composition, this is a mannered reaction to plan, programme and urban society.

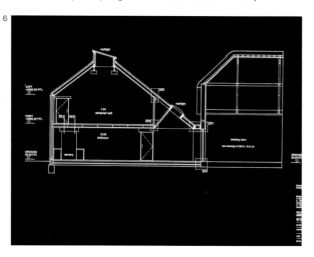

1:4.3 Detail

Architectural skill and creativity may emerge in small moments, elegantly detailed and artfully composed. The disciplined placement of air-bricks, with three verticals like miniature cricket stumps, imparts an occasional patterning within the otherwise normative brick bond. Similar games are played with the proprietary Alumasc prison system of anti-climb and anti-vandal aluminium gutters and drainpipes, which are here arranged to produce a compositional border around the whole, like a minimal picture frame.

Project 1:5	> Context and comment
Private house	> The site offers traditional domestic architecture for neighbours and wooded backlands to the rear.
Date	> The clients sought an architect with whom they could work closely, not an a priori design or predetermined style.
2002	
Location	
North London	

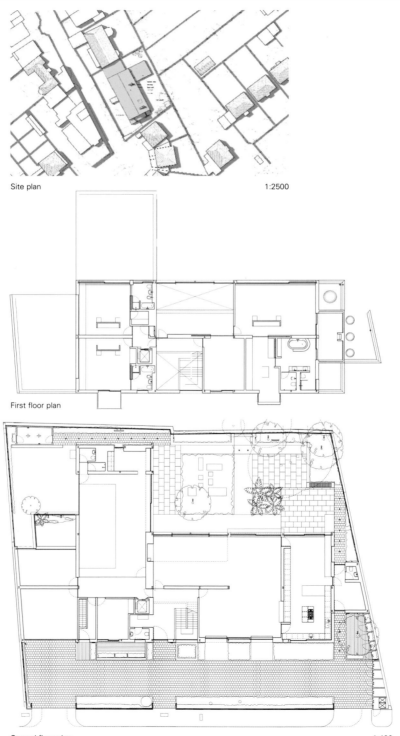

Site plan   1:2500

First floor plan

Ground floor plan   1:400

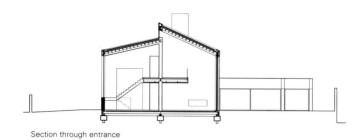

Section through entrance

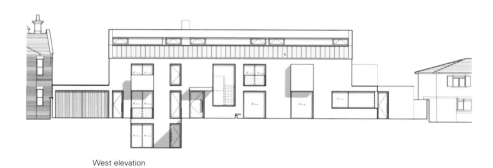

Section through pool

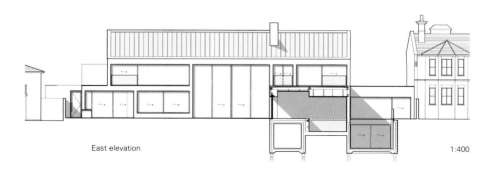

West elevation

East elevation

1:400

Fig 1 Under construction

Fig 2 View from
       back garden

Fig 3 Main bedroom

Fig 4 Street view

Fig 5 Living room

Opposite: Living room

1:5.1 Demeanour

Given the more public and formal nature of the street frontage, the front façade offers the most traditional architecture of the house: a near symmetrical composition, clad with small mosaic tiles and punctured by apertures, while the seamed zinc roof similarly responds to the roof lines of the surrounding conservation area. The overall effect is almost Georgian in its balance and quiet demeanour.

The rear is more private, and more dramatic. Large 6.5 m high windows and other extensive expanses of glass create an open grid which relates to the wooded vistas. At night, the rear facade radiates beacon-like into the darker, secluded reaches of the garden.

1:5.2 Modulation

The interior of the house is carefully modulated to meet the needs and desires of its owners and their two children.

At ground-floor level, the visitor arrives into a centrally located hall, to the left of which are hidden the pool, study, a bedroom and a number of other more private facilities. To the right of the central hall, an open plan living and entertainment zone is revealed, with its expansive rear views to the gardens emphasised by a double-height volume and massive windows.

This living and entertainment area is in turn screened off from the kitchen and family dining area by a one metre deep wall containing the video, audio and other technological requirements of modern living.

Upstairs, a split pitch section creates generous bedroom spaces, flooded with light by a front-facing clerestory window. A gallery looks back down on the living area below, and also serves to create a clear demarcation between the children's bedrooms to the north and the parents' bedroom to the south.

Project 1:6
Walsall Bus Station

Date
1995–2000

Location
Walsall

Client
Centro

> **Context and comment**

> Bus station with satellite bus-stand and adjacent public square.

> An RIBA-run international design competition, attracting over 100 entries.

> The design solution provides a single roof gathering up the programme within one perimeter (apart from a sole, small satellite canopy), with a sheltered serviced box containing toilets, plant, offices and other operational station elements.

> Outside, a new town square is created, extending away from the bus station itself to draw in a local church and connecting pedestrian routes.

> A commitment to social value is carried though to smaller, prosaic aspects of the scheme: for example, the stainless steel cubicles and uncut porcelain tiles of the toilets are of similar standard to those specified for the affluent users of the Broadgate West Health Club in central London. If it is good enough for the pampered folk of England's capital, it is good enough for anyone catching a bus home after a hard day's work in Walsall.

> Coming at the end of the early 1990s economic recession, the project provided an important financial boost to the office.

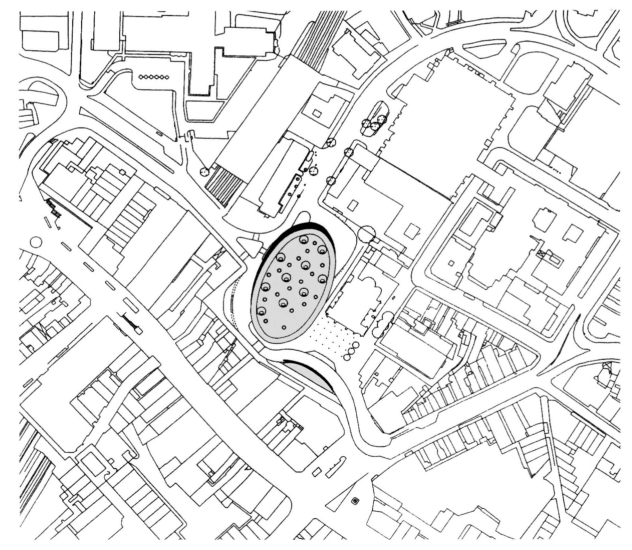

Site plan

1:2500

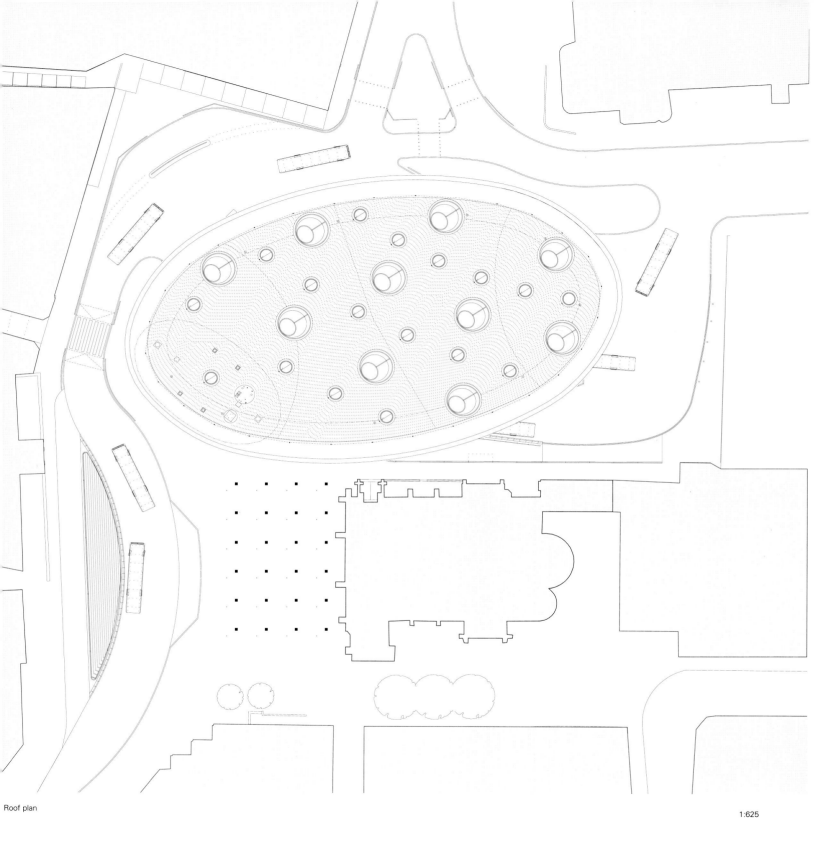

Roof plan

1:625

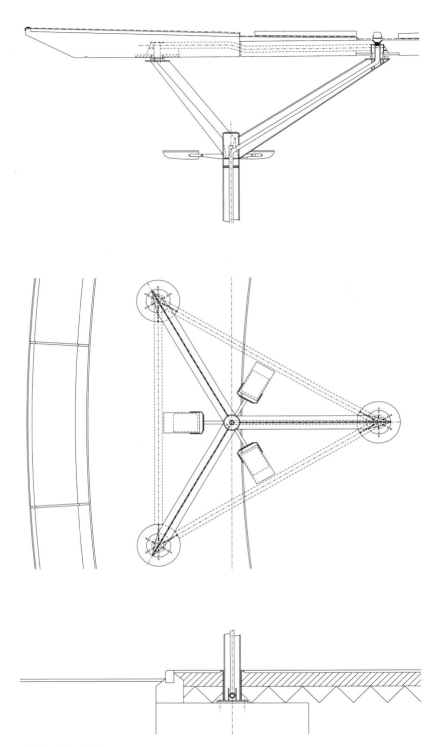

Structural tree: details

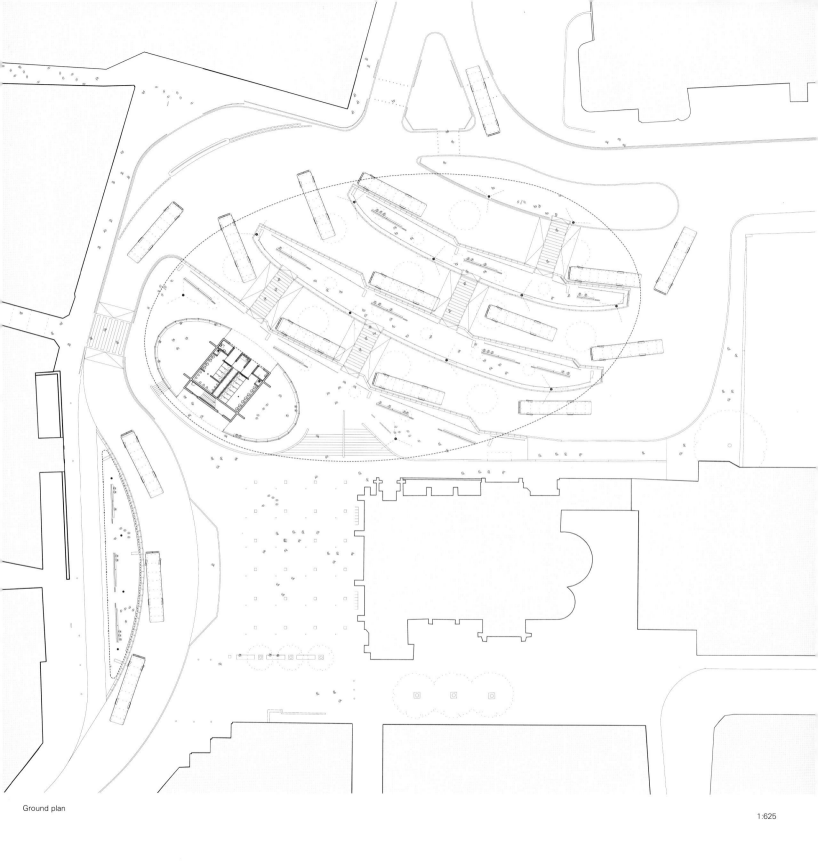

Ground plan

1:625

1

1:6.1 Analogies and metaphors

A strong geometric form reveals the scheme's origins as an instant stand-out within an intense design competition. Forceful shapes such as this one often survive far beyond their intended life, and in ways quite different to those first envisaged. Perhaps more than any other of the architects' schemes, this has certainly happened with Walsall: the office's own proposed analogies with the work of Richard Long or with a scene from Powell and Pressburger's film *A Matter of Life and Death* have given way to metaphorical comparison with, among others, a moon-base, a giant Frisbee, and, most memorably, a visiting flying saucer. All are equally acceptable – these things do not restrict a project's potential for meaning but, on the contrary, portray its connectivity with popular imagination and reception.

2

3

'FLYING SAUCER' BUS STATION PLAN

PLANS for a new £4.2 million bus station in Walsall have been unveiled.

London-based architects Alford Monaghan Morris beat competition from 101 other firms to win the commission to design the station, which will be located near St Paul's Church.

Architect Simon Alford, whose firm helped to design the futuristic RAC Control Centre on the M6 near Walsall, likened the bus station to "a discus floating in space".

An elliptical shaped roof made of steel and glass will rest on steel columns to form a giant shelter with waiting rooms at one end.

It will be lit at night and will appear to glow in the dark, said Mr Alford.

Work is due to begin late next year

STAFF REPORTER

after the details of the design have been finalised.

The project is being paid for by Centro and Walsall Council but it is hoped it may attract European Union money.

Centro, the West Midland Passenger Transport Authority, Walsall Council, Walsall City Challenge and the Royal Institute of British Architects launched the design competition in July.

Four entrants were shortlisted and interviewed before their designs were put on display in Walsall and members of the public asked for their opinions.

Centro bus services development manager John Phillips said that it was the first time an open competition had been held to design a bus station.

A spokesman for Alford Hall Monaghan Morris, which receives a £5,000 first prize towards the commission costs, said: "We are delighted to have won such a well-run competition and are looking forward to further design development of the project.

"The project represents a great opportunity for our office and we believe that when complete this prestigious commission will prove to be an important development in a vital part of Walsall."

Walsall's head of economic development Mike Kinghan said: "We are very pleased that such an excellent scheme has won the competition to build a new bus station in Walsall.

"It is very important that bus passengers have a high quality amenity to encourage the use of public transport."

1:6.2 Flows and movements

A bus station is, above all, about people and buses moving around, and the final plan discloses the building's essence as a machine for filtering movement.

With five bus companies and over 100 buses per hour, the building (and in particular the placement of the supporting steel 'trees') is essentially generated by vehicle size, movement patterns and turning circles. While the roof was originally conceived as being constructed entirely of steel, Neil Thomas of structural engineers Atelier One advised changing to a thinner canopy of concrete, with the immediate benefit of freeing up the location of the vertical supports. Other stages of the complex design procedure included the use of Autotrack software to computer model bus behaviour, before a full-scale mock-up was undertaken on railway land in nearby Dudley.

In use, the project generates a highly choreographed set of movement patterns, involving innumerable buses, visitors and travellers. Significantly, when Walsall Bus Station was celebrated in its own touring exhibition around the UK, by far the most popular and bewitching element in the show proved to be not the models or drawings but a speeded-up video showing exactly these flows and movements.

4

5

Fig 6 Early sketch by
Neil Thomas (Atelier One)
for roof cone

Fig 7 Canopy under
construction

Fig 8 Completed
roof cones

Fig 9 Canopy
from below

Fig 10 Roof cone
under construction

Overleaf:
Under construction

pp 50–51:
Interior view

pp 52–53:
New town square

1:6.3 Logic moonbase

While the underside of the station canopy has prompted comparisons with flying saucers, the upper surface with its multiple break-out of truncated cones (dispersed over a roof covering of rapidly-growing sedum) has also generated cries of similar space-theme metaphors: 'moon-base Walsall.'

Despite the drama of such sci-fi analogies, these openings have been generated by a precise logic, being calculatedly twisted to maximise light from the south, while improving summer ventilation and simultaneously keeping prevailing winds at bay. The larger openings sit over the bus routes below and are unglazed, while the smaller ones shelter pedestrians and are thus glazed for protection from rain. The latter are the maximum possible width which still allows unframed glass to be deployed, creating a condition deliberately reminiscent of the artist James Turrell, in which observers are unable to discern whether their occasional view to the sky above is natural, artificial or partially screened. Other visual games also result: from some directions the punctured holes look decidedly chaotic, whereas from other angles their ordered ranking is the dominant impression. Refer to *Interacting/Walsall Bus Station*

1:6.4 Civic space

The brooding presence of Walsall Bus Station carries with it a pervasive and insidious urban power, gathering the town into itself and so offering immediate place-marking and shelter. This civic role is accentuated during design development by the incorporation into the scheme of a section of adjoining urban fabric.

Working with landscape architect Jo Watkins, a grid of Corten steel squares is picked out from the geometry and colour of the neighbouring church of St Paul's. LED lighting sets out yet another grid. The consequence is an unexpected and unrequested gift from the architects and client to the city of Walsall – a new urban square. In relation to the bus station, it also provides an entrance of considerable luxury, that is, an entrance not as a simple door but as a piece of landscape.

London £11 day retu...

up here.

A question of timing

Architecture and its relationship to time is a topic occasionally discussed, especially by those familiar with the work of Cedric Price. What is hardly ever discussed is architecture and timing. Some of the great 'what ifs' of recent British architecture have hinged on timing: what would have happened had Peter Palumbo been able to build his Mies tower in the City of London at the time of the original exhibition in 1969, when it had broad support? What might Colin St John Wilson's British Library have been like, had not the sudden rise of the conservation movement blocked demolition of buildings opposite the British Museum originally planned on the site? And in my own case, what would the rear kitchen extension chez Finch in London SW12 have been like had we commissioned it when the AHMM practice had just started in the late 1980s, rather than when it had come to public prominence ten years later?

It would probably have been different in appearance, but not in spirit. The attitude of the practice to a modernist architecture has not changed significantly since the four partners of AHMM were absorbing the teaching of tutors like David Dunster and Jon Corpe at the Bartlett in the 1980s. Cool without spiralling into the outer reaches of minimalism, functional without obsessiveness, interested in light, materials, colour and the way a space might be used or lived in – the practice is in these attitudes not particularly different from many good firms working in London, and AHMM have always been generous in acknowledging the skills of their peers.

So what gives these architects, this firm, its particular reputation within the current profession? It is partly because AHMM does indeed see itself as part of a profession which should be (not uncritically) supported. All are members of the RIBA; the practice has given substantial amounts of time in respect of exhibition organisation, RIBA visiting boards, award- judging and committee work almost from its formation. One never has the impression that this is done in a self-serving or cynical way.

Their timing in starting the practice, and their initial choice of office location, was in retrospect a disaster. The splendid top-floor in Charlotte Street made it seem as though the firm had already achieved success when it was rubbing along on some work done in association with BDP and the occasional competition. The next location, a few streets away in Alfred Place, was no better, proving wildly expensive compared with the fee income available as the recession beginning in 1990 struck home, and young architects found themselves up against it for several years. Moving further east to Old Street in Clerkenwell was a really smart piece of timing. It coincided with the practice's increasing involvement with property clients in general and Derwent Valley, owner of their new home, in particular. There was a certain inevitability about the firm ending up remodelling the Morelands office complex, and establishing a relationship with their landlord's circle which has extended to other projects, most notably the revamping of the railway building at Paddington now occupied by Monsoon.

The practice's persistent hard work and rigorous attitude, both to design and teaching, and its development of relationships with smart contemporaries in allied worlds (for example engineering), eventually led to a series of successes, but not without doubts and uncertainties. I remember having supper with Paul Monaghan during a very dry period, and talking about the problems many good British architects had in previous generations in getting a sufficiency of projects. Shortly afterwards the Walsall Bus Station design won the international competition (impeccable timing) and the drought was over.

Looking to the wider political and economic scene, the practice has benefited from a climate in which private practice has taken on work which not so long ago would have been the province of the public sector. Would the Great Notley or Jubilee schools have been designed by a private practice? Or the Walsall bus station? On the other hand, the private sector has been tough to become established in for a firm which is not overtly 'commercial', and which by definition started with little or no evidence that it could operate successfully in the cut-throat world of business architecture.

Perhaps here, too, timing has worked to advantage. Big developers began to take a new attitude to younger architects during the 1990s, and even if at first it was the practice's design for a British Land health club rather than the office complex in which it stood which established a relationship, established it was. AHMM has also been invited to design projects for the leading patrons of contemporary housing design, the housing associations run by Peabody Trust and Rowntree Foundation, and, for both, work of unusual design power and effectiveness has resulted. More good timing, but of course you can only take advantage of timing if you have something to offer.

So: architects of skill, commitment to their profession, to teaching, to principled pragmatism (not quite the same as pragmatic principles) and to an idea of social decency rather than imposed political philosophy. It could make them sound worthy and dull. Nothing could be further from the truth. I think it is fair to say they like a party; the celebration lunch to mark the end of our kitchen extension lasted until 11pm.

Paul Finch

2:0 Surface

Architecture can be about far more than the design of a project according to an a priori scheme of form, shape or pattern. In the 'Non-style' section of Manual this thesis was explored through a myriad of tactics to do with the intimate relations of formal properties to concerns of economics and investment strategies, structural rationality, movement patterns, planning disputes, divergent social contexts, environmental awareness, innovative technologies and so forth.

In such cases, the appearance of architecture is often held to be the result of processes, conditions and reasons which lie 'behind' it. But what happens when the reverse is held, when the outermost layer of architecture is seen to be the territory of exploration? What are the possibilities of skin, graphic or colour? What about the surface of architecture?

It is worth noting immediately that the focus on surface is not necessarily a bad thing. Some critics have tried to argue that such a process inevitably leads to a reduction of architecture to the image or to the superficial, but in fact the opposite can be true. A focus on surface can lead to a richness of architectural explorations.

On the one hand, this can mean concentrating on the overt materiality of architecture, paying particular attention to such things as surface colour, light, texture, material or asperity. These attributes on their own can give much cause for delight.

On the other hand, they also lead to a profound questioning of architectural meanings. Architecture can operate as a kind of existential mirror, prompting those who experience it to reflect back on their own identity. The modulating properties of that mirror assume important performative roles: the exact nature of different surfaces leads to correspondingly diverse senses of self- and corporate identity, of spatial as well as visual experience, and of social meanings and values. The surface of architecture is not, therefore, by any means superficial, but is one of the possible moments by which architecture enters into the urban and social realm.

Project 2:1	> Context and comment
Work & Learn Zone	> Pavilion for the Millennium Dome exhibition.

Date
1999–2000

> AHMM collaborated with Tim Pyne's company WORK to produce one of the successful contributions to the exhibition.

Location
Millennium Dome,
Greenwich

> An elegant shed is animated with alternating billboard triptychs.

> Each of the three exterior images represents a different aspect of British life: print works of the Financial Times for working; rows of books for learning; and a typical countryside-park setting for something quintessentially British.

Client
New Millennium
Experience Company

> Of these three images, the bookshelves produced the most contentious debate, which spiralled out of control all the way up to ministerial level. After the great and the good spent ages choosing exactly the right edition of Proust for what was conceived as a display of 800 books, at the last minute it was realised that 1400 volumes would be required. This led to a last-ditch raid on Waterstone's bookstore, and to the final line-up where the Encyclopaedia of Goldfish Management jostled with Tolstoy.

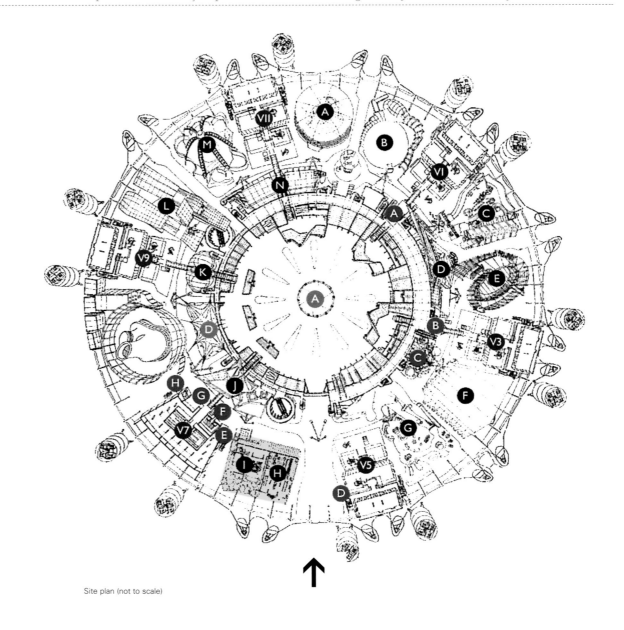

Site plan (not to scale)

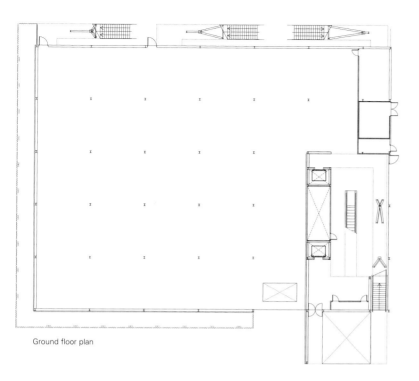

Ground floor plan

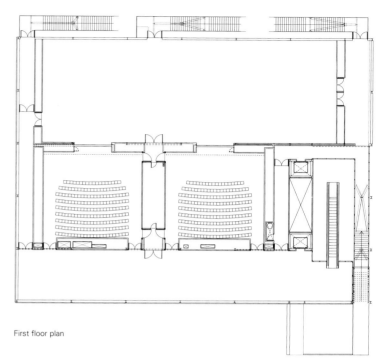

First floor plan

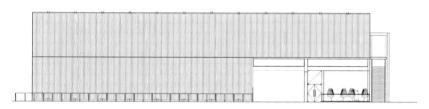

North elevation

East elevation

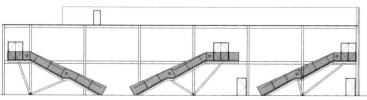

South elevation

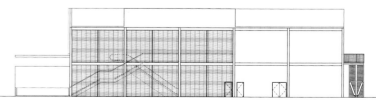

West elevation

1:500

2:1:1 Gift wrapping

After an initial idea that the Work & Learn zone might have some kind of changing façade, the decision was taken to render the entire structure into a singularly enormous picture, thus uniting what were essentially two zones ("Work" and "Learning") into one frame, and to wrap it around the corner. When set against some of the highly mannered shapes and sculptural creations of the other zones in the Millennium Dome this is a highly reductive architectural form, startling in its immediacy and bold packaging.

The technology used is essentially the same as that of a conventional, dynamic advertising hoarding, where triangular section vertical struts rotate in order to present three different images in sequence. But the Work & Learn version was by far the largest such hoarding ever constructed by its Icelandic supplier or, indeed, by anyone else in the world.

The result is to present the entirety of the structure, comprising 3520m^2 of floor space, as one giant parcel bound in fantastic paper. Visual effect here becomes more important than underlying construction, creating a condition of simplicity and intrigue, of delight at the surface and of wonder at what might lie within. It is a gift to the visiting public, and one which they alone ultimately unwrap on entering the zone.

2:1.2 Rhythm

Where graphics, imagery and architectural surfaces are brought together, this is typically undertaken under one of two conditions. On the one hand, the surface may be static, as with a super-graphic, logo or conventional billboard. On the other hand, the surface may move but only as a simple flat screen, as with giant video screens or normal dynamic billboards.

The Work & Learn zone is both of these conditions yet more. Firstly, its image wraps around the two main sides of the building, creating an enclosure and not just a screen. But more importantly this image changes, and not just in the way that a television image suddenly switches from one picture to another. Rather, at Work & Learn the images gradually roll in a linear pattern from one end to another, either as one continuous scroll, or first along the upper half and then the lower half (like an enormous raster), or indeed even from opposite ends simultaneously. The variable programming as well as the slow speed at which the images transform thus creates a temporality of unfolding quite unique to this structure. The whole effect is also heightened by the noise made by the motors and vertical struts when they rotate, adding a rasping and mobile layer of sound as it migrates across the face of the structure.

What first appears as a singular image, almost monumental in its scale and certainty, thus mutates into a far more dynamic and provisional architectural entity, one which is either one thing or another or yet another – and even sometimes something in between. This is surface as motile and fluctuating pattern, as dynamic rhythm.

2:1.3 Angel suits

In the bottom right-hand corner of the exterior sit an army of angel-winged anthropomorphic creatures, created with the help of the product design company Inflate. Each creature comes equipped with a miniature computer screen in order to play its part in a twenty-first century 'Domesday' book – the Tesco-sponsored SchoolNet 2000 – in which thousands of British school children record internet-based impressions of their local community.

In contrast to the billboard imagery of the exterior, a surface which is encountered purely by looking and listening from afar, this is a surface into which the visitor bodily steps, becoming enveloped by the welcoming wings. Once dressed in this inflatable skin, the visitor then peers into yet another surface, that of the internet screen. In that instant, they are transported away from the Work & Learn zone and out into the wider realm of the child's imagination.

Figs 1–3 Billboard phases 1,2 and 3

A Letter from Shoreditch
Hi Paul,

Sorry I couldn't be there tonight, but Iain asked me to say something about working with AHMM on the Dome. The weather here in Shoreditch is lovely as you can see, so in a post-low-fat-cappuccino Charlotte Road aura, here we go baby...

When WORK won our second and third zones on the Dome, we decided we had to build a very big shed very quickly. We were a year behind (because the lot we had taken over from had made very little headway) and the NMEC were ordering the lifts and escalators within a month.

We had no idea what was going to go in it, or what it was going to look like. New Labour were still formulating their policy on education, and, as far as work was concerned, there was an threatened recession so when the powers-that-be went to the party conference in Blackpool, they couldn't figure out if the future was rosy or dreadful.

This was a bit of a problem for us because everything had to be passed in front of a load of political committees for sign-off, and we didn't have time for all that.

We came up with the winning idea of covering the shed in the world's biggest triptych billboard – so we didn't have to get sign-off on what the building looked like for a few months until we sorted out what it needed to say. (The photo images for the outside would only take three weeks to produce, albeit in Iceland because for some reason they own the world's biggest photocopier or whatever it is). What we didn't need was a prima-donna architecture outfit to work with us, so I called Paul (a fellow Scouser), and before we knew it we were in meetings every day with the likes of David Puttnam and the chairmen of Tesco and Manpower.

With a palpable sigh of relief NMEC signed off the triptych idea and (courtesy of AHMM) the very big, 3,700 m², steel and concrete frame started to go up about a month later.

It was a bit weird seeing all the chauffeur-driven limos parked up outside our office in Shoreditch, but it was all quite rock'n'roll. At one stage, Alicia, Paul's wife, started to refer to me as his 'other girlfriend' because we were spending so much time in the pub talking about the Dome (and she was having to deal with the mess which rolled in afterwards).

Within about a minute of WORK or AHMM issuing a drawing, it was being fabricated; there's no such thing as an extension of time in the exhibitions world anyway, but the millennium was probably the world's most immovable deadline.

We used to go to Clerkenwell to crit AHMM's architecture, and they came to Shoreditch (which is much cooler) to crit our exhibitions, usually over several beers. Both companies respected each other (well, they said they did) and when the RIBA gave us an award (the first ever for an exhibition), the judges said the relationship between the building and the exhibition was 'seamless.'

We got it finished second and third of all the zones in the Dome. First, of course, was our other one (and OK, fourth was ours, too.)

Shame it all ended up as landfill.

As far as we are concerned, AHMM are the dog's.

Tim Pyne

Project 2:2
Walsall Bus Station

> Context and comment
> Refer to *Non-Style/Walsall Bus Station*

Fig 1 Manifestation
      designs by
      Alex Hartley &
      Tania Kovats

Fig 2 Glass panels with
      white roundels

Fig 3 Walsall resident

Fig 4 12 hours –
      23 March 2001

2:2.1 Field

Beyond its elliptical roof, the architecture of Walsall
Bus Station offers a choreographic performance of
buses, people, birds and wind. In order to maintain
an architectural presence among such complex
movements, a series of precise interventions are
introduced. Artists Alex Hartley & Tania Kovats and
graphic designers Atelier Works placed a range of
deceptively simple devices: staggered glass panels
with white roundels, colour coded bus-stop and
information boards, and low concrete walls. In
complete contrast to Broadgate Club West, where
almost the entire architecture is structured around a
single surface element, Walsall Bus Station contains
a scattering of dispersed surface elements, each
making tiny yet significant adjustments to the
movements and comprehension of passing travellers;
they do not announce their presence loudly but cajole
and insinuate. This is surface as a field of suggestions.

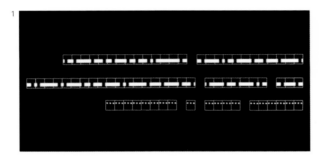

4

Project 2:3
Live-In Room House

> Context and comment
> Refer to *Non-Style/Live-In Room House.*

Fig 1 Desk diary which
       provided the Tintin
       source imagery

Fig 2 Cartoon representation
       of Live-In Room
       House interior

Fig 3 Letters between
       AHMM and the
       Hergé Foundation

Fig 4 Cartoon representation
       of the Live-In Room
       House, with Tintin figures
       reversed left to right.

2:3.1 Cartoon
Architecture can, of course, be literally reduced to surface when represented in a two-dimensional image. The particular form of the cartoon tends to emphasise surface flatness more than any other form of representation, reliant as it is on the application of colour in flat areas and on the deployment of relatively simple lines.

In images for the Live-In Room House – which began as a highly experimentalist proposition – the cartoon form is used to accentuate the project's unreality even further. As the Live-In Room House was intended for public display in the 'New British Architecture' exhibition, these cartoons succeeded well in intensifying the narrative quality of the proposal, and hence communicating its theoretical qualities to a non-professional audience.

This process occurs in a number of ways, most obviously in the various figures which populate the images: Hergé's world-famous invention Tintin and other associated characters such as Snowy, Captain Haddock and Bianca Castafiore. This tactic immediately marries the unreal and the strange (the cartoon, the total glass architecture) with the real and the familiar (Tintin and the typology of the house) into one hybrid, pictorial world, one which is at once comforting and challenging.

This image has been taken from the works of Hergé and has been modified and used with apologies to The Hergé Foundation

The exact manipulation of the characters and their stage-set adds more to this condition. Most obviously, characters talk to each other and, by implication, draw the spectator into what are presented as welcoming, lively scenes. In a more subtle process, a humorous sense of irony emerges when one notices, for example, that the boy in the night-time interior view is playing with what appears to be a model railway carriage; in fact, it is AHMM's own Poolhouse, complete with the figure of a swimmer which the boy holds up to an inquisitive Bianca Castafiore. Similarly, in the day-time exterior view Captain Haddock grunts out one of his typically expletive exclamation marks at the sight of the extraordinary house, this architecture being dematerialised to such a high degree that it all but disappears against the dramatic, mountainous background.

These kinds of imaging tactics do, of course, have certain risks attached. The cartoons' publication provoked a swift legal response from the Hergé Foundation, keen to protect the integrity of Hergé's original creations. The matter was, however, amicably resolved.

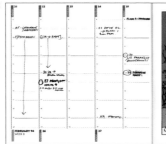

3

Dear Philippa Warhurst,
Re: Young British Architects and Tintin

I apologise for the problems we have
caused you and I will write a letter to
Nick Rodwell of The Hergé Foundation
under seperate cover apologising for
using a corrupted 'Tintin' image without
requesting their permission.

I have printed the following amended
version of the caption you proposed.
'This image has been taken from the
works of Hergé and has been modified
and used with apologies to The
Hergé Foundation' and I trust that
this is satisfactory.

Yours sincerely
Simon Allford

Dear Sir
Re: TINTIN

Thank you for your kind letter dated
13th May 1994. Please do not hesitate
to visit us, should you ever decide to
come to Brussels. It will be a pleasure
to show around the Foundation.
Best Wishes.

Yours sincerely,

Nick Rodwell, cc. Phillipa Warhurst.

4

This image has been taken from the works of Hergé and has been modified and used with apologies to The Hergé Foundation

Project 2:4	> Context and comment
Granada Television	> Office refurbishment.

Date
1999–2000

Location
London

Client
Granada Television

> Granada Television, one the UK's largest media companies, was occupying the top two floors of a nineteenth century building in central London. The new fit-out has to appeal to the creative, young-blood individuals who populate the world of broadcasting.

> Spatially, the office is opened by a simple process of cutting out a central void through the two floors.

> Around this space, a series of new ideas about offices are prototyped, particularly the manipulation of surfaces with graphics, colour and text.

1

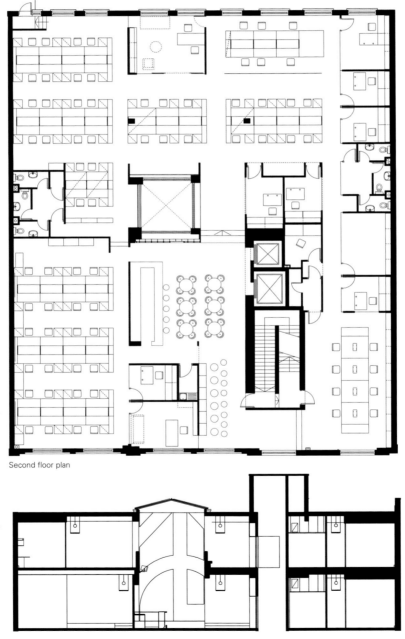

Second floor plan

Section through reception   1:250

2:4.1 No logo?

Into the central void space a giant bas-relief version of the Granada logo is introduced, constructed from plaster on framework as a semi-permanent insertion into the architecture. Yet so large is this logo – rising from alongside the bar level below to the main conference room above – that it is never fully comprehensible in one entirety; visible only in partial fragments, it is constituted as a whole not by any singular glance but only from a multiple set of views assembled in the viewer's mind.

This is an important condition, which has significant consequences not just perceptually but also socially. The viewer has a more ambiguous relationship to the logo, never dominated by its looming totality, but always reminded of the intrinsic bonds between institution and employee. The logo is there but not there, and by implication, the contractual bond is similarly present but not fixed.

The collaboration with Studio Myerscough – with whom the office worked for all this graphic work at Granada – is particularly evident in certain textual and architectural conjunctures, and nowhere more so than on the low wall in front of the lifts and on the higher wall behind the bar. On both these surfaces runs a continuous text which dryly lists the titles of Granada's programmes: Better Homes, University Challenge, Coronation Street, The Royle Family and so on. Set in capitals, devoid of punctuation and differentiated solely by colour and tone, these programme names provide a textual wallpaper, a constant yet subtle reminder that what matters in the end is no single person's ego or career but the creative product.

The tactic is particularly evident in the video sequences which Studio Myerscough created for continuous display in the more public areas of the office. Again, the obvious – straight footage of programmes – is avoided, and these alternative clips show instead a sequence of subtly manipulated and treated images, each intimating programmes as ideas and on-going moods rather than as finite moments. Like the programme titling, this is video as wallpaper, undoubtedly present yet in a diffuse and subliminal manner.

Fig 1 Exterior of existing building

Fig 2 Original Granada logo

Fig 3 Detail of video sequence by Studio Myerscough

Fig 4 Bas-relief Granada logo

Fig 5 Central void at upper level

Fig 6 Detail of video sequence by Studio Myerscough

2:4.2 Wallpaper

Similar yet different tactics are also deployed in relation to Granada's main products: the television programmes which it commissions, produces and broadcasts. Normally broadcasters deal with this kind of promotion through a series of portraits showing the stars of the shows. At Granada a different attitude is adopted.

7

8

Fig 7 Work space

Fig 8 Directional
        floor graphics

Fig 9 Glazing to offices

        Opposite:
        Bar with
        programme listing

2:4.3 Direction

Graphics can also be forthright and, as with Broadgate Club West, signage at Granada is laid on to the floor in order to guide visitors and newcomers. Although usefully literal and instructive, such signage also contains an element of surprise, its positioning at ground level creating an immediate correlation between itself and the feet of the visitor, whose animation the signage is ultimately seeking to direct.

Not all the graphics at Granada involve words. A bespoke screen and partition glazing system was researched by the architects, with glass glued directly onto the timber frames in order to create a continuous surface into which doors are then accurately punched. In the office areas, colour-coded light boxes illuminate the end of the rows of desks.

Granada, with its play of surfaces as architectural and graphic manipulation, becomes a theatre not only for the production of programmes but also of companies and creative workers. It animates products, lives and careers.

9

Project 2:5	> Context and comment
Morelands	> Refurbishment of a 1930s light industrial complex into office and retail facilities.

Date
1998

> Morelands is of direct significance to Allford Hall Monaghan Morris, as home to their own office since 1995.

Location
Clerkenwell

> Soon after becoming tenants, the architects were asked by Morelands' owner, Simon Silver of Derwent Valley Properties, and by David Rosen of Pilcher Hershman letting agents, to refurbish the whole scheme: a densely convoluted site of disparate blocks, alleys and entrances.

Client
Derwent Valley
Properties

> The architectural response involved sealing off all but one entrance, cleaning up the fabric and generally tidying up the industrial architecture. These surface moves are deceptively simple, almost giving the appearance that nothing has been done.

> Morelands is currently a popular location for architects, product designers, graphic designers, photographers and publishers; AHMM's neighbours have included Magnum, Inflate and Jasper Morrison.

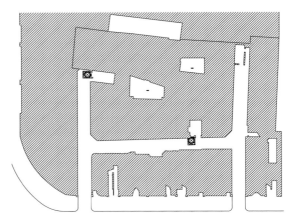

Ground floor plan – as found

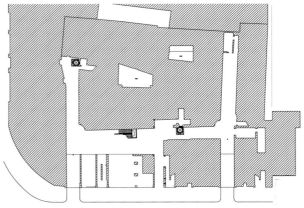

Ground floor plan – as built   1:1000

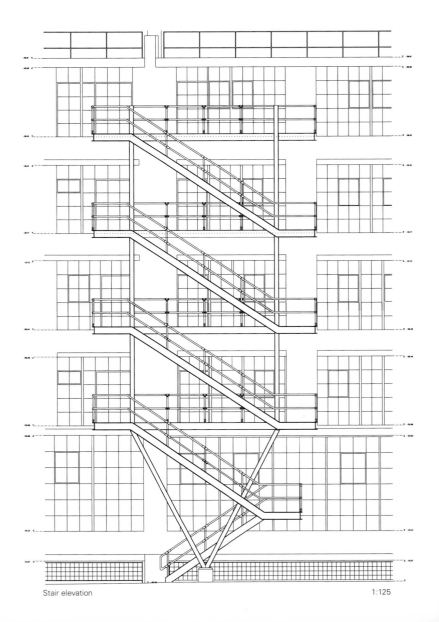

Stair elevation   1:125

Fig 1 Gated entrance

Fig 2 Stencilled
window graphic

Fig 3 Inner courtyard
and lift tower

Fig 4 Off-the-shelf
industrial staircase

Fig 5 Old Street façade,
before and after
refurbishment

Fig 6 Stencilled fire
exit graphic

2:5.1 Grain

Originally constructed in stages between 1905 and 1940, Morelands' first occupants were the rag-trade, watchmakers, engravers and printers of the Clerkenwell district, each requiring rapid individual access for the constant delivery of materials and dispatch of merchandise. The response to the rather different current tenants has been to maintain, wherever possible, the essential grain of this layout, while providing for their more modern urban needs. Thus the many entrances have been reduced to one, all original staircases have been kept (one has been turned around) while an extra, main staircase has also been added. The latter is an off-the-shelf industrial system, suitably tough but well specified for the feel of the light-industrial courtyard.

In short, this is a collegiate gatehouse-and-staircases solution, with a new identity created for the scheme as a totality. Steel lift shafts have been re-clad in order to identify each individual five-storey block. The result is a new interpretation of the industrial quarter, both fitting within yet subtly re-working the existing architecture.

2:5.2 Patina

Morelands has what can be best described as *feel* – a kind of smoky atmospherics. In order to preserve this intangible characteristic of the scheme, a deliberate choice was made to work with the extant urban patina by cleaning the raw brick and stone, scraping down fire escapes and emphasising the large metal windows by repainting them in the existing blue colour. Into this palette of surfaces and materials others have been woven in, such as the pressed metal panels used for the lift towers and the packing-case, stencil-style graphics stencilled upon them by graphic designers Studio Myerscough. The idiosyncratic yet highly successful deflection of these numbers to the very edge of the tower panels was a suggestion not of the architects or graphic designers but of the client – in any case, it shows the importance of fine-tuning every detail of this type of scheme.

These tactics have important financial as well as aesthetic results. When the AHMM office first moved in to Morelands the property was renting out at £2.50 per square foot per annum. Through considered refurbishment – focusing on surface, grain and patina rather than on dramatic intrusions – it was hoped to realise £12.50 to £15. In fact, by 2001 the scheme was commanding a peak of £32.50 per square foot.

Project 2:6	> **Context and comment**
Dalston Lane	> Apartment block offering affordable rental accommodation.

Date
1998–99

> Above 750m² of retail space sit 18 residential units (12 x 2-bedroom, 6 x 1-bedroom). Each apartment boasts a south-facing balcony which, at 15m², is larger than Peabody's requirement for a living room.

Location
Hackney

> Other features include double-height entrance spaces and fantastic window views over London, carefully modulated by Okalux screens.

Client
Peabody Trust

> As with the CASPAR scheme in Birmingham, Dalston Lane has been commissioned within the context of an acute shortage of affordable housing. It is rented to local residents who earn below a certain salary, and is neither subsidised by nor profit-making for Peabody.

> The combination of high design quality with relatively low rents ensures the scheme is extremely popular, not least with young architects.

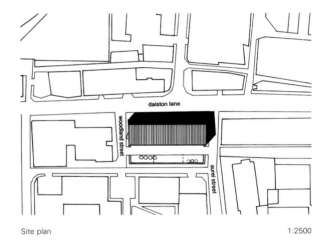

Site plan   1:2500

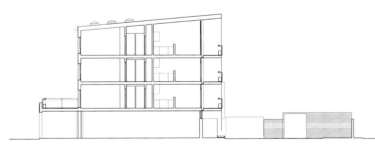

Cross section through flats

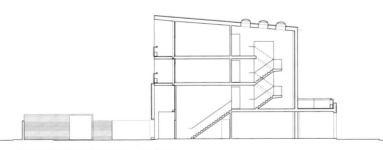

Cross section through entrance and staircase

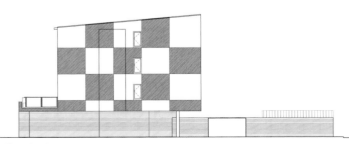

West elevation

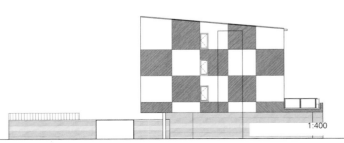

East elevation   1:400

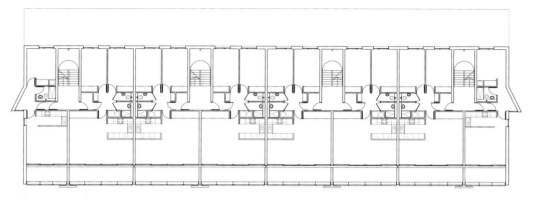

Second and third floor plan

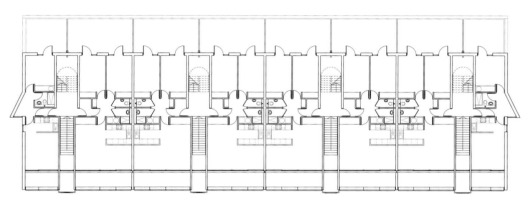

First floor plan

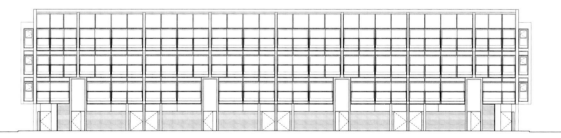

South elevation

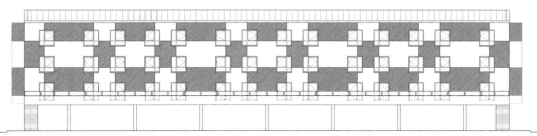

North elevation   1:400

Fig 1 Apartment balcony

Fig 2 Battenburg cake

Fig 3 Lutyens' Page
Street and Vincent
Street housing
(1928–1930)

Fig 4 Apartment living
room, with view
south modulated
by Okalux panels

Fig 5 North elevation
from Dalston Lane

Fig 6 Surface grid
pattern aligned
with window
mullions and transoms

Fig 7 South elevation

Opposite:
Flank wall with
ceramic brick
at ground level

2:6.1 Camouflage

The most compelling aspect of Dalston Lane is its surface treatment. In the context of this grim and down-at-heel part of the London Borough of Hackney, the decision to drape the building in a massive blue-and-white chequer-board grid is decidedly courageous.

In fact, there are skilful urban logics at work here. Primarily, far from shouting out its presence, the checkerboard serves to break down the mass and scale of the single block to something much more in keeping with the variegated jumble which constitutes the rest of Dalston Lane. Within this grid, nuances of patterning come into play, such as its neat yet unexpected alignment with window mullions and transoms rather than frames, or the way in which it bends around onto the building sides, or is deflected onto oriel windows, or is picked up by the blue of ceramic bricks at ground level, or is reflected in the horizontal landscape planting pattern, or is reflected yet again by the Okalux grid of the apartment windows… All these arrangements add up to form a surface pattern that is at once compellingly simple yet subtly complex – architecture as urban camouflage.

2:6.2 Cake and icing

For the devotee of British architecture, references to Edwin Lutyens' late-1920s housing at Page Street and Vincent Street in London add resonance to the Dalston Lane scheme. Local residents, however, prefer a more direct comparison: with the Battenberg cake, whose cheerily unexpected gridded section provides an undeniably apt metaphor. (This metaphor is not always, however, meant kindly. Refer to *Interacting/Dalston Lane*). There is also a partly philosophic, partly practical, partly pedantic discussion about the Dalston Lane chequer-board pattern. Is it, the question demands, truly a pattern which lies only on the surface? For what appears to be paint, and hence something laid on top of the "real" architecture, is in fact coloured render, and so penetrates several millimetres down into the building. Conversely, that coloured render is only the top coat, and thus does not reach all the way down.

The answer is not clear, and is not perhaps ultimately important, except to point out the very ambiguity of what might be said to constitute surface at all. Certainly, like the icing on a splendiferous cake, if you were to pick it all off you might find that you had no real cake at all.

Project 2:7	> Context and comment
Crown Street Buildings	> Apartment plus retail and commercial facilities.
Date	> An important triangular site, next to Cuthbert Brodrick's elliptical Corn Exchange and the
2000–02	White Cloth Hall in a central Leeds conservation area.
Location	> The winner of a limited competition, the design stitches together two vacant sides with
Leeds	existing Victorian buildings.
Client	> A four-storey block of apartments sits over ground-floor retail and commercial outlets.
Welbeck Land	A central first-floor courtyard provides private open space for residents.

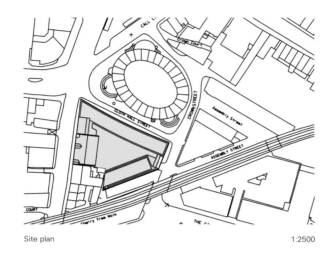

Site plan   1:2500

First floor plan   1:400

North elevation

West elevation

South elevation

1:400

2:7.1 Armadillo

The treatment of the external elevations is extremely robust, taking cues from the surrounding Victorian warehouse architecture. Smooth, hard bricks emphasised by deep window reveals create a regimented framework of masonry structure; a respectful but never fawning nod at the muscular architectural environs of Leeds.

This brick framework is an armour, an armadillo's skin of horny scales raised as defence against both harsh weather and determined assailants.

2:7.2 Chameleon

At once more subtle and more dramatic is a different aspect of Crown Street Buildings: its chameleon-like mutation from yellow through green to blue. This gradual migration of colour is played out along the large faïence panels fronting each apartment.

Where the brick framework is solid and constant, this ceramic counterpoint is provisional and transitory, a reminder that even buildings change according to time, view and disposition. This piece of architecture never quite looks the same.

Fig 1 The Corn Exchange

Fig 2 Study for façade

Fig 3 Model view
       from west

Fig 4 Under construction

Fig 5 Schematic diagram
       for façade
       colour system

Fig 6 Façade unfolded
       to illustrate
       colour range

       Opposite:
       Model view

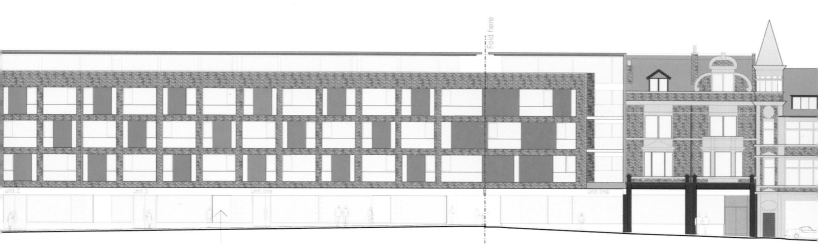

Fold here

Project 2:8
Broadgate Club West

Date
1997–98

Location
West End, London

Client
Broadgate Club Plc
The British Land
Company Plc

> Context and comment

> New health club as sister facility to the already successful Broadgate Club in the City area of London.

> Both large (over 2,000 m²) and up-market, Broadgate Club West is highly distinct from the pop-in and pump-up buzz of a conventional gym: the modernist hotel elegance of the reception yields to more traditional changing rooms, while the dynamic atmosphere of the exercise zone is carefully screened from the calmness of the adjacent bar.

> The office argued for an architecture which operated within the context of the initial and continuing marketing of the facility as much as within normal architectural parameters of cost, construction, function, and experience.

> Situated on the ground floor of Triton Square, designed by Arup Associates.

> Apart from the Poolhouse this was the office's first large job with a sizeable budget.

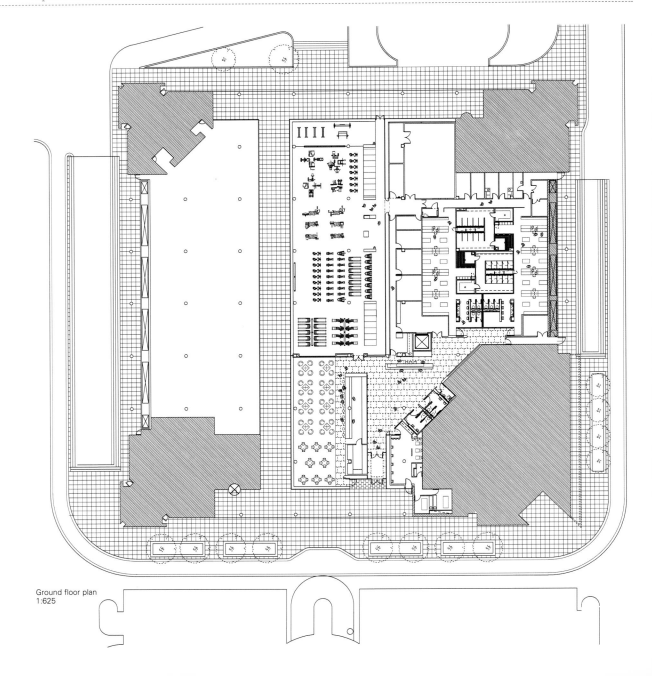

Ground floor plan
1:625

THE BROADGATE CLUB

Fig 1 'Colourflow'
system within
the illuminated
spine wall

Fig 2 *The Architects'
Journal* (1998)
front cover

Fig 3 Different colour
states of the
illuminated wall

Fig 4 Howard Hodgkin
mural at the original
Broadgate Club

2:8.1 Spine and guts

Given the clear demarcation spatially as well as atmospherically between the different functional zones of the facility, the importance of Broadgate Club West's most dominant architectural element – a coloured and illuminated spine wall – is self-evident. Running the entire length of the scheme, this spine separates changing rooms from the exercise zone, proceeds to wrap around conceptually onto the front surface of the reception desk, and then re-emerges at the front of the scheme as a prominent addition to the exterior. The whole plane of the wall controls the entirety of the project; one surface dominates the architecture.

A closer, internal inspection reveals the complex construction of this essential spine. The "Colourflow" system adopted was originally designed for the flooring of 1970s discos, and consists of blue, pink and green cathode tubes sandwiched into a 600mm-deep space, skinned with glass and opal inter-layers to aid colour diffusion. Stepping into this interstitial space is like entering into the very guts of the project. The whole thing can then be programmed to give blue, pink or green lighting, or even a slowly mutating psychedelic variation of the three. What at first appears as a thin skin is thus revealed, on closer inspection, to be a thick layer, a zone of technological intensity and source of emanating presence.

2:8.2 Wash and glow

Internally, this is a deliberate reference to the Howard Hodgkin mural used at the original Broadgate Club in the financial district of London. While pooled areas of light or, conversely, complete flatness of colour were alternative possibilities for the wall, the architects encouraged a more subtle middle way. The result is a slight yet unmistakeable Rothko-esque effect, a subtle modulation of colour over surface which is richer and more interesting to the eye even if not immediately evident to all except the most curious of viewers.

2:8.3 Mirror and body

While most gyms comprise a set of equipment surrounded by a wall of mirrors, Broadgate Club West is effectively the reverse, with windows and walls on all four sides and a set of free-standing steel-framed mirrors distributed among the equipment. These mirrors help to disperse the presence of the illuminated spine wall, each reflection setting up its own miniature clone and so further invigorating the space with its radiant presence. The interior becomes fractured, multiple, alive.

The result is a swimming pool-like penetration, each club member being infused with the light and mood emanating from the illuminated wall and its reflective siblings. This heightened bodily state is then carefully maintained in the changing room materials, where warm-to-the-touch Corian benches and handrails (designed by Andrew Stafford) provide comfort to naked flesh, and deep blue tiles and individual mirrors play similar attention to bodily peace and privacy.

2:8.4 Face and mask

Outside, the external element of the illuminated wall projects into the outside world. This is the most extrovert element of Broadgate Club West, the radiant light creating a powerful colouristic disjunction into the otherwise grey tones of the surrounding London context. It is the most public face of its surface architecture.

I LOVE THE REST OF MY LIFE
THOUGH IT IS TRANSITORY
LIKE A LIGHT AZURE MORNING GLORY.

Fig 5 Gym interior

Fig 6 Bench designed for
the Broadgate Club
by Andrew Stafford

Fig 7 Broadgate Club
promotional literature
featuring Haiku poems

Fig 8 Changing room

Fig 9 View of gym
from arcade

Fig 10 Floor graphics

Around the corner, a somewhat different surface tactic operates: a horizontal sequence of windows and coloured panels allows club members to look out, while a balancing series of linear portholes lets passers-by glance inwards without encouraging gawping or voyeuristic gazing.

Produced in collaboration with the graphic designers Studio Myerscough, these masking screens are further variegated by the inscription of haikus. The poems emphasise bodily or health-oriented themes and so refer to the activities of club members but the screens face outwards (and so ultimately cater for those on the exterior of the project). In contrast to the coloured face at the front, this is the modulated mask of the project, a carefully choreographed set of rules which at once encourage, allow and deny visibility.

2:8.5 Poetry and promotion

The haiku poems also form part of yet another surface strategy at Broadgate Club West, this time to do with textual and graphic branding. During the marketing phase of the club, some of the same haikus appeared in the brochure, advertisements and other promotional materials, as did the logo for the scheme, the flaming torch standing sentinel by the main entrance.

Within the gym interior, Studio Myerscough's graphics appear on both floors and columns, thus helping to distinguish between different zones of activity but also reinforcing the connection between surface and message and between architecture and marketing.

3.0 Getting things done

Allford Hall Monaghan Morris was founded in 1989, at the beginning of the long economic recession that continued into the middle of the next decade. Faced with these kind of circumstances, many architecture practices – particularly those with four partners – split up to allow each member to fend for themselves. AHMM did the opposite, maintaining the core of the partners, a real office and a team of other people with their own expertise and obsessions.

Hence the early 1990s saw the office undertake a wide range of things, from the design of the smallest architectural projects, to product design, building facility management, weekend ideas competitions, hack journalism and even an appearance with Chris Evans on Big Breakfast's 'One Lump or Two' game. Over a decade later, while much of this activity is best forgotten, a surprising amount is still worthy of some attention in its own right.

Above all, what such activity shows is that there is great value to be had in 'getting things done', even if the product may be of unknown immediate value. An inventive architectural practice will possess a facility for finding good things in unexpected places, for producing, for example, elegant pieces of furniture together with thought-provoking conceptual ideas, experimental prototypes, surprising urban insertions and substantial cultural documents. Where some might prefer to wait for the perfect commission, other architects will opt to test their mettle in a disparate field of activities, getting things written, spoken, taught, drawn, discussed, noticed and built within the wider public field.

For the AHMM office, one result has been that the architectural output often far outstrips the normal definition of architecture as drawings, books and well funded buildings. In this oeuvre we therefore find a multi-disciplinary range of products which, taken together, test the definition of architectural practice.

Project 3:1
Paternoster Alternative

> Context and comment

> Theoretical design for an exhibition on alternative strategies for the Paternoster site.

Date
1990

> Soon after they formed, AHMM joined a series of conversations with a disparate range of London-based practices. One important topic concerned the prestigious and contentious Paternoster site next to London's St Paul's, where the William Holford-designed offices – a powerful but now run-down symbol of post-war modernism – were possibly to be replaced by a neo-historicist scheme being put forward by John Simpson, Demetri Porphyrios and Hammond, Beeby & Babka. The group containing AHMM undertook to make a counter-proposition for public display at the Architecture Foundation.

Location
Architecture
Foundation

Client
N/A

> AHMM's contribution consists simply of a set of photocopy collages. Each collage provides a conceptual critique of St Paul's, the existing and the proposed Paternoster development, and indeed the very idea of public space and monuments.

> The reworking of images of St Paul's is in part contingent upon the now-iconic status of St. Paul's Cathedral, as most famously demonstrated by Herbert Mason's much-reproduced photograph of St Paul's during the air-raids of World War II.

> The uncertain, Terry Gilliam-esque quality of the somewhat rough-and-ready Paternoster images can also be discerned in the later cartoon-style representations of Live-In Room House (Refer to *Surface/Live-In Room House*).

> Experimenting with rapid use of the photocopier led to a subtle shift in the office's working practices, moving away from drawings which immediately try to show exactly how a building would look, to more suggestive images intimating how the architectural idea might develop.

> The rise of the photocopier was an integral part of the development of architectural practice at this time. Sarkpoint, a fledgling reprographics firm in north London, quickly became one of the most important foci for this activity, a place not only where new designs and competition entries were reproduced, but where architectural gossip was exchanged, design students hung out and friendships were forged.

Fig 1 Photocopier

Fig 2 St Paul's Cathedral,
London (29 December 1940),
photographed by Herbert
Mason. (The monochrome
original has been retouched
in this version, to add the
fake colour of flames)

Opposite:
Paternoster City

3

3:1.1 Paternoster City
Given that Holford's existing development had enjoyed glowing testimonials from the likes of John Summerson and Nikolaus Pevsner, and given that it contained a significantly lower density than the new proposal by Simpson et al, could it really be considered to be all that bad? Indeed, what would happen if the scheme were cloned and stamped right across the face of London? Would it even matter if, as happens here, the entire west face of St Paul's were removed?

3:1.2 Piazza del Duomo
In total opposition to *Paternoster City* is the *Piazza del Duomo*, an obvious parody of the renaissance piazzas of Pisa and Florence, replete with a giant campanile composed from the stacked forms of the nearby Standard Chartered Bank. The sheer vastness of the resultant open space begs the question as to what such civic gestures might actually be for. Is public space simply open space with nothing in it?

3:1.3 Fun Fair City
Fun Fair City offers one possible answer to *Piazza del Duomo*, placing a fantastic fairground on a car park-like site. The Ferris wheel is borrowed from Carol Reed's 1949 film *The Third Man*, creating a knowing tension between the seemingly carnivalesque atmosphere of anti-profit fun and the more overtly financial motivations of tourist spectacles and property development. Who has the right to use the city? And what forms of entertainment and pleasure can be encouraged?

3:1.4 Pavarotti in the Pulpit
Similar critiques occur in the fourth image of the series, where the religious usage and free-to-enter access of St Paul's are replaced by a paying concert by a popular entertainer. Why not, the proposition asks, let St Paul's be a secular public amenity?

3:1.5 Dome
Most radical of all is the proposal to reduce St Paul's to nothing more than its great dome, and to simply keep that dome raised up in the sky on giant props. The proposition is ruthlessly direct: all that ultimately matters about St Paul's is the distant view of the church as monument. Partially a critique of the dominance of spectacle over locality, and with apologies to Cedric Price's earlier suggestion for the chimneys of Battersea Power Station, *Dome* also questions the attitude among certain parts of the conservation lobby to cherry-pick certain 'special' or 'exceptional' buildings at the expense of architecture or the city as a whole.

4

Optimistic worlds

If one lined up a selection of architects in an identity parade, one is unlikely to pick out the four partners of Allford Hall Monaghan Morris. The recipe for this partnership is ingenious. Take a second generation architect about town with a penchant for late-night conversation, wine and red meat, combine it with a forthright Scouser with a sentimental side and an interest in contemporary TV, an encyclopaedic knowledge of 70s and 80s glam and what the Americans call power rock. Mix this with a concoction of highly particular public school boy with a preoccupation for pensions, law and the nags. Add the final component: a sensible, steady-handed master of critical paths, programmes and big-time construction with a few quirks I don't know about (let's face it no one's perfect) and you have the very unique cocktail that is AHMM. Together this team has all architectural bases covered; they have the ability to land, design, run, publicise and batter the client or contractor if they get out of order. This is the key to their success.

The world of AHMM is optimistic. They can make things happen, and not dwell on problems but solve them and move on. Snatched conversational vignettes often give an insight into their supportive yet creative world. It takes risks, bites-the-hand-that-feeds and makes sure that their work is equitable to clients, users and passing public – these are no capitalist lapdogs.

But it wasn't always like this. I first met them in the late 1980s at the various venues around town which attracted the young, the ambitious and the eager-to-network. One such venue was the old 9H gallery, or rather the pub opposite as the 9H exhibitions were, let us say, a little turgid. They were either just finishing working as a team at Building Design Partnership or had just set up their office. A year or two before that they had graduated from the Bartlett School of Architecture and, before that, had done undergraduate work at Sheffield and Bristol. One must remember that the broken husk of the Bartlett was still shambling on, and this was a time before the Cookian revolution which soon after started to rejuvenate its ragged reputation. The fact that AHMM retained their creative optimism during this period and did not descend into a cynical, knowing, academic, lacuna of production is extraordinary. It is a testament to them that they straddle the professional world of corporate doings and the strangely invaginated world of academia.

They had an office in Charlotte Street and later moved opposite Cedric Price's office in Alfred Place. The Alfred Place location for me and them was a touchstone in the architectural firmament, being close to the master as well as the West End girls, dos and pubs. At first business was slow and the early 90s recession hit them hard, but they were resilient, buoyed up by the Poolhouse commission and a healthy scavenger attitude. That recession badly damaged my generation's hopes of success and many fledgling interesting partnerships bit the dirt, and the dirt tasted bad. The Poolhouse and its dogged development and concern for every detail was to be the catalyst for the beginning of their acceptance into the corporate world and their future success.

Allford and Monaghan have been teaching at the Bartlett longer than any one else involved in design. Their Unit 10 is characterised by a philanthropic interest in students, and by an attitude that seeks to get students to create their own work and maintain the self confidence to carry it off. Their teaching in recent years, in direct contrast to my own, for example, seeks to actively subvert existing planning protocols, regulations and received wisdom of contemporary practice. Students are required to use these restrictions as creative opportunities, allowing them to create new takes on educational buildings, homes and leisure activity which exploit these arcane architectural rules of engagement. The work is surprising and always thoughtful. This useful strategy teaches students that everywhere is an opportunity, not a straitjacket.

My generation has spectacularly failed to deliver an architecture appropriate for our contemporary existence, and it has often reverted to the fatuous arguments, ideas and concepts of a defunct bunch of old duffers. AHMM are actively open to change and work in collaboration with, and not against, the old guard – this, I suspect, is an often dirty job, and I'm glad they are doing it.

This daily struggle to educate, influence, create and live is conducted in an office atmosphere that is without the usual ego, hierarchy, stupid hissy fits and wanky sophism of some of the more well-known offices. I love them dearly. Respect them and I'm proud that they are my friends. Even when a friend of mine headbutted a friend of theirs, they were philosophical. We have fun together and our drinks, eats and chats are a grateful punctuation to my life, and I hope to their lives too.

Neil Spiller

Project 3:2
Melvin Apartment

Date
1992

Location
Waterloo

Client
Jeremy Melvin

> **Context and comment**
> Private apartment.

> Despite a budget of only £22,000 for the total refurbishment of a small two-bedroom residence, the Melvin Apartment became a project of considerable importance to the firm: it was the first time they built and published something which allowed the investigation of real architectural design in the context of economic constraint, prototyping, marketing and communication.

> Originally designed for Jeremy Melvin, a friend of the four partners, the apartment was later acquired as the private residence of Paul Monaghan and his family.

> AHMM's own contribution to the Under 50K exhibition. [Refer to *Getting things done/Under 50K*]

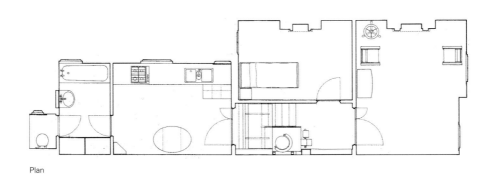

Plan

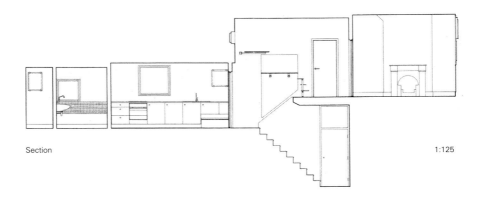

Section   1:125

3:2.1 Ring-fence

The most important decision in the Melvin Apartment is an economic one: to ring-fence 15% of the budget for a single innovative gesture. An elevated steel and glass platform-cum-desk is inserted into the void over the stairway. The desk surface, made from a sandwich of glass and honeycomb aluminium, acts as a horizontal vitrine, transposing the objects above into a collection of mysterious silhouettes. The right-hand element of the steps, a cantilevered vertical glass sheet relates to the Live-In Room House proposition.

Spatially, the platform/desk shows the benefits of thinking volumetrically rather than in plan, in effect squeezing a study into what is already a very compact apartment. This element became the hallmark of the project, the single idea which people latched on to as something which they too could replicate either as a direct copy or in spirit. It is "both ingenious and uplifting," wrote Hugh Pearman, the *Sunday Times* architecture critic, "all for much less than half of the £50K. It made me positively envious."

3:2.2 St Jerome in his study

The client is an architectural critic, historian and educator with a specialist knowledge of German philosophy. The notion of the platform/desk as a kind of semi-separate territory for intellectual endeavour was thus important to the essence of the scheme. To this end, a metaphorical allusion is drawn to 'St Jerome in His Study', a painting by Antonello da Messina, a major Italian painter of the *quattrocento*, and much discussed by art historians for its rich symbolic content. The comparison not only gives the impression that the client occupies both architecture and canvas, but that the flat itself shares the contemplative air evident in Antonello's artistic invention.

3:2.3 Cover star

Despite, or perhaps because of, these rarefied associations, the Melvin Apartment has become one of the most publicised of all of the practice's projects, appearing not only in the architectural press but in many other publications. These range from heavyweight newspapers like the *Financial Times* and *Independent on Sunday* to popular interior design magazines like *Elle Decoration* and Terence Conran's *The Essential House Book*. Beside the obvious importance of this kind of profile-raising material early on in an architectural practice's life, getting the Melvin Apartment published in as many different places as possible became something of a game for the office to pursue. Perhaps its appearance here in *Manual* will mark the end of this series, but probably not…

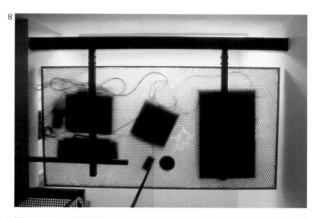

Project 3:3	**> Context and comment**
Under 50K	> Exhibition showcasing schemes costing less than £50,000.
Date	> Getting to know the firms involved in the Paternoster discussions led AHMM to propose
1992	another venture of benefit to younger architectural practices: an exhibition of small-budget
	projects, proving how architect-designed constructions could not only be affordable but
	actually save the client money.
Location	
RIBA, London	> Extending this concept into the exhibition process itself, central costs were kept down by requiring
	each practice to provide their own display material within a given set of design parameters.
Client	
RIBA	

3:3.1 Value

Against the then-current public perception that architects are an expensive luxury, *Under 50K* shows the reverse to be true, that employing an architect can actually lead to a value-for-money product. The decision to set a ceiling of £50,000 – a figure within the imagination of many domestic as well as corporate clients – makes this point all the more real.

3:3.2 Career

The exhibition served to promote the careers of both well-known and lesser-known architects, most of whom have gone on to become established members of the national and international architectural scene. Over 30 firms and individuals participated in the project.

3:3.3 Professional role

Under 50K was held at Gallery 2 in the RIBA, a facility overseen by Kate Trant, and inaugurated a whole series of exhibitions curated by AHMM in that location over the next two years. Without payment (and often acknowledgement), the AHMM office initiated such exhibitions as *Before and after planning* and *Before and after design & build*, *Designing for doctors*, *Strangely Familiar*, *Tasty* and *How did they do that?*. None were highly elaborate affairs, but each posited a different, provocative assertion about the role of the contemporary architectural profession.

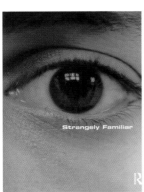

Fig 1 *How did they do that?* exhibition poster

Fig 2 *Tasty*, exhibition pamphlet

Fig 3 *Strangely Familiar*, exhibition catalogue

Fig 4 *Under 50K*, exhibition poster

Under 50K. Projects with a contract value of less than fifty thousand pounds. At the RIBA second floor gallery 5 November to 24 November open from 10am until 6pm Mondays to Fridays and 10am until 1pm on Saturdays. Allford Hall Monaghan Morris. Apicella Associates. AO Partnership. Pierre d'Avoine. Birds Portchmouth Russum. Tim Bushe. Brady Mallalieu. Caruso St John. David Chipperfield. Simon Conder. Peter Davidson. Mark Dudek. Jonathan Ellis-Miller. Robert Evans. Hawkins Brown. Trevor Horne. Hutton Sauerbruch. Maccreanor Lavington. Mackenzie Wheeler. Manser Associates. David Mikhail. Munkenbeck and Marshall. Patel Taylor. Matthew Priestman. Sergison Bates. Katherine Shonfield. SW Architects Ltd. Tower 151. Wigglesworth and Butler. Jonathan Woolf.

Private View Monday 9th November 1992 6pm to 9pm

Ordinary/Extraordinary

One of the keys to Allford Hall Monaghan Morris' work lies in their particular understanding of the city. Even before their collaboration started at the Bartlett in the mid 1980s they had experienced gritty urban life, in Liverpool, Sheffield, Bristol and London, cities whose complexity and neglect were made manifest in the riots of 1981, when each of the partners were undergraduates. Fortunately the Bartlett provided fertile ground for reacting positively to these urban challenges, in the studio teaching of David Dunster and Jon Corpe. Dunster projected an enthusiasm for Aldo Rossi which gave an intellectual focus to Corpe's daemonic pragmatism.

For AHM and M this suggested a dual approach. Cities were indeed worthy objects of intellectual speculation, but they were also, equally and simultaneously, susceptible to pragmatic intervention. Throughout their work practicalities are never divorced from concepts, nor do they dominate: rather there is a flow, which may not be entirely smooth, predictable in its outcome, or universally successful, between idea and reality.

From this balance between pragmatics and imagination comes an inherent flexibility, a flexibility which remains principled rather than the pawn of clients' or planners' whims, and which allows invention in form, detail and use of material without referring it to some chimeric 'Committee of Taste'. Similarly flexibility feeds into their model of practice, a necessary quality in variable economic times and when there are four partners.

The advantages of their approach to work were foreshadowed in their first collaboration, the 'Fifth Man' diploma project with its implication that working together made more than the sum of the parts (though there were other reasons behind the choice of title). However it has grown into a way of perceiving the challenges and opportunities which come their way. Rather as 'Capability' Brown acquired his nickname from his habit of looking at a dull stretch of ancestral acres which the latest minor aristo wanted to 'improve', and commenting on its 'capabilities', AHMM look at unpromising pieces of urbanism, the back end of a bus station, an etiolated upper-floor flat, the dual-entranced Barbican or a backland dairy, and see in them possibilities for betterment. They do not look for the ordinary where it does not exist, nor do they praise it for its own sake. Instead they look for the inherent possibilities of a site and its programme, and seek to develop an architectural form from that. For them every project is simultaneously ordinary and extraordinary as a condition of being, not something which substitutes for solving a problem or capitalising on opportunity.

Of course this may leave them open to the charge of being opportunists. But they could reply that the portfolio of work over their first decade and a half shows a willingness to address some of the most fundamental problems facing urban life: transport, education and key-worker housing. Now, with projects like the Barbican Centre, they have the chance to show that they can bring the fruits of previous endeavours together in the public realm.

Jeremy Melvin

Project 3:4	> Context and comment
Halas Archive	> Conversion of an existing garage into archive and studio facilities.

Date
1994

> The client, John Halas, was a film animator and pupil of Moholy-Nagy at the Bauhaus. The existing house was designed by the Czech architect Kubick, a pupil of Erich Mendelsohn.

Location
Hampstead

> The commission, with only £30,000 available, called for the conversion of the stand-alone garage into a new storage facility for Halas' irreplaceable films, as well as to create a new studio area within which he could work.

Client
John Halas

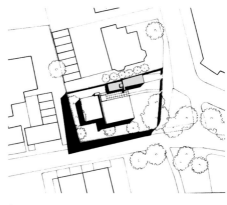

Site plan   1:1250

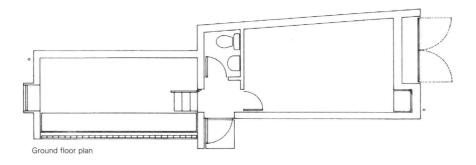

Ground floor plan

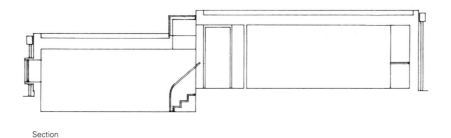

Section

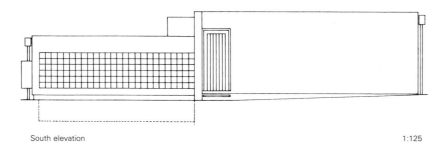

South elevation   1:125

3:4.1 Dummy

Rather than retain the existing garage, the building is made from a pair of contrasting new elements. A dark box replaces the demolished garage and provides the windowless and thermally stable archive, with dummy 'garage' doors (actually shielding a small store) retained in order to gain planning permission. A light box is added at the rear, forming a studio flooded with light from a long glass-block window wall.

3:4.2 Minimal

The archive's appearance is largely determined by the highly restrictive budget. Hence the glass-block wall is the largest possible without having to resort to the use of reinforcement, while simple internal finishes include painted blockwork, grey floor screed and MDF stairs and workbench. Standard, economic materials are used throughout, except for the purpose-designed aluminium hoppers and downpipes.

Fig 1 Drawing of archive featuring 'Max and Moritz' and John Halas

Fig 2 Studio interior

Fig 3 External view

Project 3:5
St Mary's Nursery
School

Date
1996

Location
Kilburn

Client
The Roman Catholic
Diocese of Westminster

> **Context and comment**

> A small nursery school in the Kilburn area of London.

> The design is the result of a carefully crafted plan, strongly edited views, and a few sculpted elements scaled for both adults and young children.

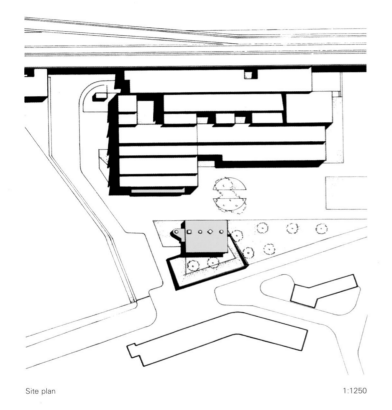

Site plan   1:1250

Ground floor plan   1:250

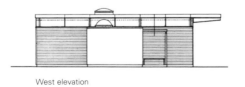

West elevation

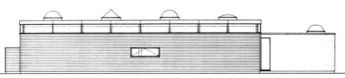

North elevation

South elevation

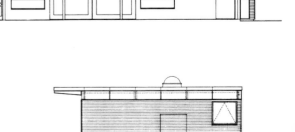

East elevation   1:250

Fig 1 The building
when completed

Fig 2 English garden
as inspiration
for the secret garden

Fig 3 School revisited,
2002

Fig 4 Classroom
interior

Fig 5 Exterior
in winter

Fig 6 Classroom
interior

3:5.1 Cold call

Perhaps the most interesting aspect of this project is how the commission was gained in the first place. After completing a small project for the London Borough of Brent's Reading Recovery Centre, the office decided to try to move into the educational market. A letter to 150 London schools extolling the virtues of the Reading Recovery Centre led to a new job re-organising the interior of St Mary's School using a bespoke plywood panel system. The reconfiguration of the school allowed an annexe to be sold, which in turn funded the building of the new nursery – for which AHMM were recommended by the headmaster as architects. The commission for a new building – only their second full in-the-round building – was thus duly won, the consequence of a simple but determined chain of events involving two modest pieces of internal design, a pile of letters and, above all, a willingness to get out there and get some work.

3:5.2 Terrain

Despite a tiny budget, a small amount of money was found to employ Jo Watkins for the landscaping. The intention was to create a secret garden, offering the children somewhere to play while being screened and secluded behind a green wall of hedges.

Project 3:6
Millennium Products

Date
1999–2000

Location
Various sites world-
wide

Client
British Council
Design Council

> **Context and comment**
> Transportable exhibition pavilion.

> As part of the millennium celebrations, the British Council and Design Council commissioned an exhibition pavilion to promote innovative UK-designed products around the world.

> Destinations included Brunei, Singapore, S. Korea, Australia, Japan and India, where it was viewed by tens of thousands of visitors.

> Millennium Products rejects the common exhibition device of simply displaying products on plinths, preferring instead to enhance and communicate products' qualities through a range of spatial, visual and haptic tactics, all contained within a tight 16.3 x 6m floor zone.

> Apart from the design – by AHMM in collaboration with Studio Myerscough – members of the team were also responsible for the pavilion's repeated assembly, maintenance and disassembly.

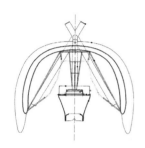

Video booth: plan

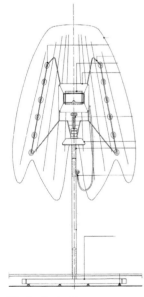

Video booth: elevation

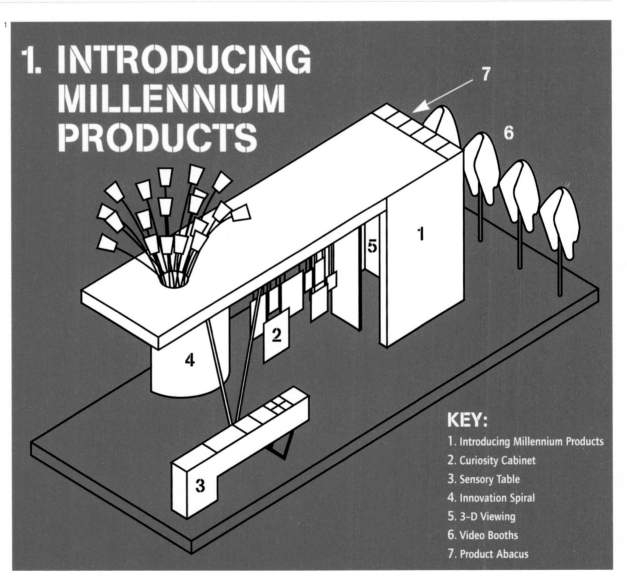

1. INTRODUCING MILLENNIUM PRODUCTS

KEY:
1. Introducing Millennium Products
2. Curiosity Cabinet
3. Sensory Table
4. Innovation Spiral
5. 3-D Viewing
6. Video Booths
7. Product Abacus

OUR SELVES   OUR PLACES   OUR WORLD

3:6.1 Touch
A table of touching encourages visitors to sniff, smell, grope and feel the temperature of different products. The table is placed at child height, and exhibits are accessed via holes in Perspex covers, through which they can be handled using protective gloves.

3:6.2 Body seduction
For the 'innovation spiral', a floating screen combined with floor graphics leads the visitor into the heart of this element. Bodily movement is seduced, not forced, just as a flower's petals manoeuvre a bee towards the pollen within.

3:6.3 Metaphor
Four inflatable-wing-plus-video-screen devices (precursors to those at the Work & Learn zone) perform a similar role, enticing the visitor to become enfolded in a clothing-like construction. The theatrical and metaphoric nature of these pavilion elements, designed by the office with Velvet Air and Inflate, proved highly successful in holding the visitor's attention: angels, NASA suits, camera tripods, inflatable toys, submarine periscopes and aeroplane journeys (the screen technology was adapted from a Virgin Atlantic 747) are all possible associations.

3:6.4 Spectacle
A large 3-D video shows products such as the Lotus Elise and Ford Ka cars, objects too big to bring physically onto the pavilion. The visitor is once again enfolded, this time by the visual spectacle of the surrounding imagery.

3:6.5 Abacus
One wall contains a huge range of products, displayed photographically in horizontal series, like an abacus. Scanning a barcode (using one of Tesco's hand-held 'Inside Trak' scanners, itself a Millennium Product), lets the visitor access more detailed information.

3:6.6 Curiosity cabinet
A twenty-first century version of the curiosity cabinet is created by the office and Inflate, shrink-wrapping and tagging all of the items in display. Presenting all items in this homogeneous manner infers that all of them are 'products' – even such things as prosthetic legs or radiators.

Fig 1 Exhibition catalogue

Fig 2 Millennium Products logo
       by Johnson Banks

Fig 3 Peter Mandelson
       tests a product

Fig 4 Pavilion in Singapore

Fig 5 Video extract: Lotus Elise

Fig 6 Shrink-wrapped products

Fig 7 Inflatable wings
       and video screens

Fig 8 Innovation spiral

Fig 9 Image taken from
       A Matter of Life and Death,
       Powell and Pressburger (1946)

Following pages:
The Touching Table

Project 3:7	> **Context and comment**
Corn Exchange Hoarding	> A competition was advertised in Design Week magazine for a temporary hoarding to be placed in front of a speculative office building, then being constructed by British Land. Although conceptual and art-based hoardings are now commonplace, in 1995 this was an innovative move by a developer.
Date 1995	
	> AHMM and Studio Myerscough proposed a massive 215 ft-long, two-tier construction with an upper zone of huge direction-dependent graphics, and a lower zone of more detailed information.
Location St Marks Lane, City of London	
	> Over £50,000 was spent on what is, of course, in the end simply a temporary screen, but which when placed in situ created a dramatic and controversial urban intervention.
Client The British Land Company Plc	> The office describe the Corn Exchange hoarding as their longest, thinnest building.
	> The competition win helped inaugurate a relationship with The British Land Company, which later worked with AHMM as client for Broadgate Club West and for their own headquarters office.

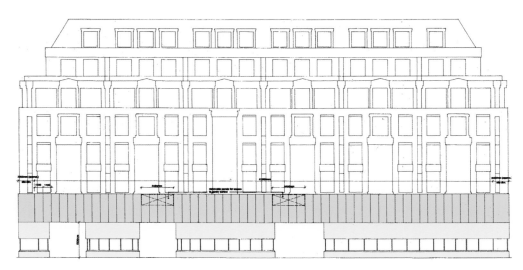

Elevation   1:500

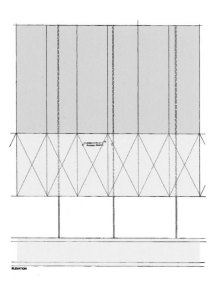

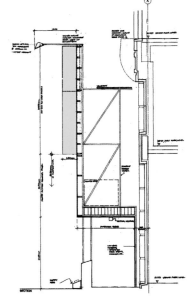

Bay elevation   Section   1:125

Fig 1 Air France, Piccadilly

Fig 2 The completed building

Fig 3 Hoarding detail

Fig 1 Walkway
        level artwork

Fig 2 Walkway
        level view

Fig 3 Photographs
        by Trevor Key

        Top: View from north

        Opposite, top: View from south

3:7.1 Viewpoints

How do you exploit an acutely sideways view? This was the primary question for the Corn Exchange hoarding which from one angle displays a series of cryptic vividly-coloured images, each relating to one of the five senses: a music cassette for sound, roses for smell, a dog for sight, corn on the cob for taste, an iron for touch and so on. From the opposite angle the hoarding appears quite differently, and simply spells out the word Familiarity in huge white-on-black letters.

How long does it take for something new to become familiar? The power of this simple visual device is hard to impart on paper. Set in the narrow site of Mark Lane, the hoarding not only inserts a giant, over-scaled piece of colour into a dark back alley, but City workers, surprised at first seeing the giant graphic during their morning commute in from Fenchurch Street or Tower Hill stations, are then on their return journey doubly taken back by its reversed and altered face.

3:7.2 Is this art?

The hoarding's photographs are by Trevor Key, previously responsible for the album cover of Mike Oldfield's *Tubular Bells*. One depicts the most highly paid dog in the UK, a placid-tempered Pug whose contemplative eyes and wrinkled skin form a hyper-realist portrait good enough for any gallery. Others concurred, and a section of the

2

hoarding, complete with traces of London traffic fumes and scattered pigeon droppings, was later exhibited at the RIBA, while a bas-relief model and accompanying photographs made an appearance in the Royal Academy Summer Show.

The City of London had another opinion, particularly as the hoarding had been built without planning permission. "We are not against avant-garde art," stated Peter Rees, the chief planning officer, "but this is ugly… it's a cacophony that's drawing unnecessary attention to a building site." (After much wrangling, the hoarding stayed put for its full six-month life).

3:7.3 Local sensibility

The Corn Exchange office building under construction, designed by Fitzroy Robinson, had no pre-let tenant. In order to help sell the building, the lower-tier of the hoarding follows through with the theme of senses, this time connecting them to the immediate locality. This section of the hoarding thus operates as a form of neighbourhood rebranding, helping passers-by to discover or re-acquaint themselves with forgotten parts of the City. The poetic and suggestive nature of these textual elements – written by journalist Tom Dyckhoff – acts as a more intimate counterpoint to the dynamic and forceful super-graphics up above.

4.0 Landing

How does architecture relate to the earth on which it sits? What are the correspondences at once physical (immediate positioning), ideational (philosophical conceptualisation) and environmental (consideration of the sustainable) between architecture and its landscape? What is the 'landing' process by which a building comes to take its place within, and impart its presence upon, the world?

There are, of course, architectures which have located such considerations at their very heart. One concern has been to place buildings in careful relation to the rural or natural landscape, while a more urbanistic version of the same approach involves a relation to streetscape and the hard fabric of the city. More philosophically, the Heideggerean notion of architecture emphasises building as a way of making and dwelling in the world, while, perhaps most commonly known of all, is the environmentalist concern with energy, particularly as it is actually consumed or symbolised within the final building. But these are highly specialist procedures, sometimes mobilised by their architects in an overtly focused manner, even to the exclusion or detriment of other aspects of architecture.

Another approach is to keep such concerns explicitly in the foreground, while simultaneously balancing them as part of the architectural agenda as a whole. For example, there is an increasing realisation that architecture is not always about building structures anew at all times and occasions, and that architecture can also profitably and successfully use the existing fabric of the city as an opportunity for creative action. This is, of course, indicative of an attitude towards sustainability which is beginning to inform large sections of the architectural profession – sustainability as a positive impulse, helping to mould the potential and architectural qualities of the project. This, then, is landing the building as total design response rather than as single-issue manifesto.

Landing is, therefore, necessarily a holistic intention rather than a detail-specific activity. Nonetheless, it must involve some highly focused architectural tactics, engaging with vision and materiality, scale and form, design and production as well as with experience and phenomenological encounter. The schemes presented here demonstrate exactly these kinds of concerns.

Project 4:1
Great Notley
Primary School

Date
1997

Location
Great Notley, Essex

Client
Essex County Council
Design Council

> Context and comment

> Primary school, with additional requirements regarding energy-efficiency and sustainability.

> In the county of Essex, developer Countryside Properties have built a new garden-village style development – some 2,000 homes in various kinds of faux vernacular and historical styles, ready for occupation by well-heeled commuters. As part of this development, called Great Notley, a new primary school is required, with 180 places for local children.

> The 1997 competition brief, set by Essex County Council and the Design Council, added an extra agenda to that normally set by a primary school, calling for a prototypical architectural response to the demands of the 1992 Rio Earth Summit: an energy-efficient and sustainable school which addressed how buildings are conceived, constructed and inhabited, while costing no more than a conventional product.

> The winning entry by AHMM, Atelier One and Atelier Ten, from 90 entrants, sought to delineate an approach to the building rather than to immediately create a design proposal.

> Great Notley recognises that in the most fundamental manner no new building can ever be truly sustainable; in making a new building new ground is always taken away, and enormous amounts of energy are always expended in terms of construction, materials, equipment production, sourcing and maintenance. Great Notley therefore knowingly interacts with land, energy and environmental factors while also maintaining high design quality.

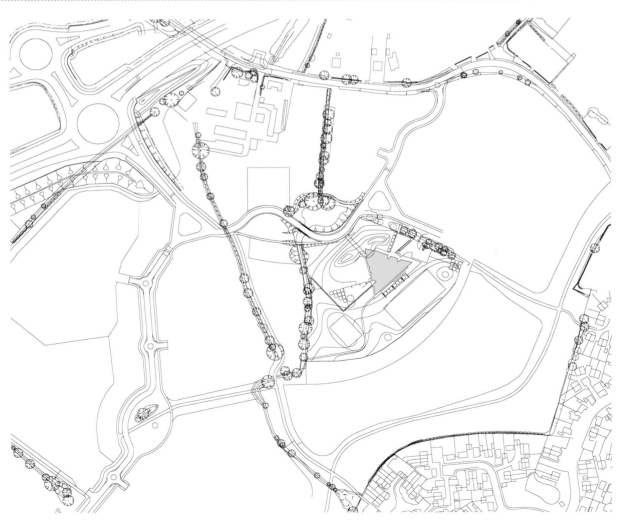

Site plan

1:4000

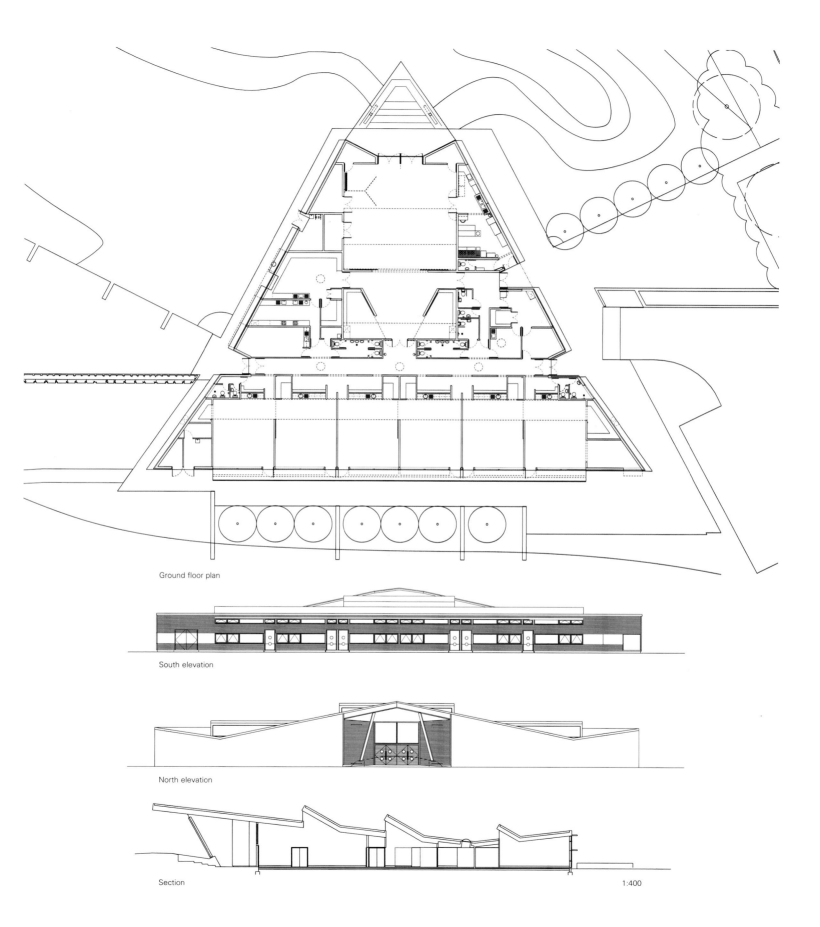

Ground floor plan

South elevation

North elevation

Section   1:400

I've been readin'
that some of our school is made in Sweden

I've heard tales
that some of our school is made in Wales

I've heard there's a chance
that some of our school is made in France

I'm bubbling to tell you…I can't wait…
but…some of it comes from the United States

I'm not a spoilsport but I think it sounds finer
that some of our school is made in China

Believe it or not
some of it's Scots

If you go to meetings,
if you go to talks,
I think you'll hear
that bits are from Yorks.

Floors, roofs, windows, doors
Gutters, wires, worktops, nails,
Yorkshire, and the USA,
France, China, Scotland, Wales.

Michael Rosen
(commissioned for Great Notley School by
the Design Council)

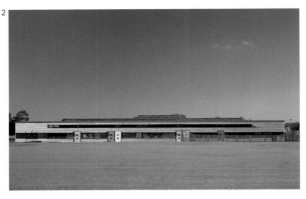

4:1.1 The law of diminishing returns

The first tactic adopted on the greenfield site of
Great Notley was that of rejection: unlike most
self-avowedly 'sustainable' architectural projects,
Great Notley eschews such things as serried banks
of photo-voltaic cells, spinning wind turbines, or
medievalesque aesthetics.

These kinds of thing often make only marginal sense
in terms of energy; once the embodied energy
required to actually make them and the time that they
are likely to be in operation is taken into account, the
energy savings are often nowhere near as large as is
promised. Furthermore, and just as importantly,
the high capital cost of many 'environmentally friendly'
devices renders them unviable in real-world
architectural applications, useful only as visual
gimmicks. Great Notley's services engineer, long-time
collaborator Patrick Bellew of Atelier Ten, calls this
the 'law of diminishing returns', a warning which is
taken seriously at Great Notley.

4:1.2 Materials and devices

That Great Notley succeeds in being environmentally
conscious is evident from its low annual energy
costs. How this is achieved comes not from high
capital investment but from the careful consideration
of materials and environmental devices which do
indeed render the school properly sustainable –
sustainable, that is, not necessarily in terms of pure
energy creation, but through purchase, maintenance
and long-term environmental auditing.

Great Notley consequently incorporates, for example,
Warmcel insulation (partially manufactured from
recycled paper), linoleum (made from linseed oil
and jute), and compressed bamboo floorboards
from China. Wherever possible, recycled plastics
replace PVC, as in the work surfaces moulded from
compressed plastic bottles and which insert a
highly appropriate multi-coloured disjunction into

the children's classrooms. This strategy is also applied
to environmental engineering, as with the natural air
brought in at ground level from the outside and
circulated out again through roof-light structures.
The arrangement is a way of avoiding deep-plan air
conditioning while at the same time increasing natural
light in the school.

4:1.3 Microclimate

Also of environmental significance is Great Notley's
'grass' roof, whose naturalistic appearance masks
a sophisticated package of mat-grown sedums on
a geotech fabric underlay. This device transforms
the building's microclimate, welcoming butterflies
and birds, provoking a changing aesthetic (the palette
of greens and browns turns a delightfully flowered
red each spring), and protecting the roof membrane
from UV degradation.

Interestingly, there is also another accidental benefit
which accrues to the use of a grass roof: it is this
sedum pelt which provides one of key images of
the school, frequently chosen by the media as a
readily-comprehensible symbol of sustainability.

4:1.4 The triangle approximates the circle

What is perhaps Great Notley's most significant
achievement lies in an aspect of architecture that
is not always readily associated with sustainability,
but whose nonetheless critical centrality to the
environmental success of the project illustrates
the office's mode of architectural invention and
problem-solving: the plan.

For Buckminster Fuller, the sphere is it. At Great
Notley, the triangle is it. The whole building is
contained within this distinctive form (although
a splaying-out at the southern corners and a
tucking-in ofthe northern nose means the
three sides are not quite pure), allowing for an
optimisation of floor/wall ratios, room orientation,
available sunlight, low energy emissions and
comprehensible spatial arrangement.

According to one of the practice's typically idiosyncratic
aphorisms, this optimisation process is one where 'the
triangle approximates the circle.' While this aphorism is
certainly inaccurate in mathematical terms (a triangle
and a circle are in fact as geometrically opposite as
possible), its logic nonetheless succeeds in conveying

a number of key benefits, ranging from economics (the paring back of the 1080m^2 total area initially budgeted for by the client to the actual 990m^2 of the school released 90m^2 of value back into the core budget for other purposes) to energy efficiency (every classroom has a southern orientation). To give one more specific example, by all but erasing the plan area normally given over to corridors and circulation space in a school great savings are made in terms of money and energy.

Great Notley takes its sustainability seriously, integrating environmentalist concerns wholly within the architectural project in order to enhance, not compromise, its qualities. The school shows that sustainable architecture is not just for extreme sustainable projects – it has grown up, moved on, and become part of the everyday process of architectural design.

4:1.5 Farmyards and stealth bombers
Despite its determinedly environmentalist agenda, Great Notley Primary School also bears witness to another office concern, namely that although sustainability is an important consideration, if the building is not a delight to use, then it is a failure. If it is not a pleasure for school kids, for people who teach in it, for people who pass by, it is not truly 'sustainable' at all. In short, it has to be used

the overall intent of the scheme, i.e. that the triangular form maximises architectural and environmental benefits in the same way that the circle encompasses maximum internal area within a minimum perimeter. The purely spatial aspects of this arrangement are dealt with elsewhere (Refer to *Spacing/Great Notley Primary School*), but in support of this reasoning, consider that in environmental terms the triangle yields

Allford Hall Monaghan Morris
Morris Allford Monaghan Hall
Monaghan Morris Hall and Allford
How about that? I remember them all.

Are we looking at four people here?
Or is it one person with a four-name name?
Maybe it's two people with two names each?
If so, are they different? Or are they the same?

I think Allford is someone old and grand
I don't think they can find Mr Hall.
I think Monaghan comes from Ireland
I think Morris is rather small.

Allford Hall Monaghan Morris
Morris Allford Monaghan Hall
I think one of them's also called Peter.
I wonder if one of them's also called Paul…

Monaghan Monaghan Morris and Morris
Allford Allford Hall and Hall
Morris and Monaghan, Hall and Allford
There! Look at that! I've remembered them all.

Michael Rosen
(commissioned for Great Notley School by the
Design Council)

Fig 6 Classroom elevation:
  detail

Fig 7 The prow

Fig 8 Classroom
  interior

  Pages 120–121:
  View from the west

This concern with the Vitruvian category of 'delight' is readily apparent at Great Notley. The Plimsoll line banding over the windows first originated as an ordering device for the various apertures, creating an abstract yet nautical *fenêtre longue* which in turn provided enough metaphorical strength to suggest the deployment of porthole windows. Yet the banding also aids in emphasising the horizontality of the landscape, against which the rises and falls of the building become more noticeable, thus reinforcing the school's appearance as a ship gliding across the surrounding greenery. Elements like the projecting canopy for the main entrance play a supporting role, doing their own bit to bring ground into dialogue with architecture.

At a larger scale, looking at the site as a whole, the school emerges as one of series of such incidents in the landscape – either shapes (triangle as school, ellipse as ball court, rectangle as sports pitch) or conditions (play, work, garden, meadow). The total landscape becomes controlled in the way in which a farmyard is controlled: partially haphazard, partially incidental, but always delineated and finite. It is very much a project which makes its own landscape and site.

The overall effect of this school architecture is strikingly ambiguous: uniquely modern yet contextually sited, familiar yet odd. And despite an overtly modernist language, the combination of black Plimsoll band and main cedar cladding alludes to the black bitumen barns common to this part of the world. This kind of paradox is something which the four partners admire in all architecture, and not just their own projects, and conversations with them frequently make their way to discussions about the strangeness of buildings and, in particular, how when visiting a building of great quality, it frequently seems to be either bigger, smaller, or somehow weirdly at variance from the plans or photographs. In short, good architecture has something which marks it out as different.

In their own work the office now accepts the architectural problem for what it is and designs accordingly. As for Great Notley, sited close to the false historicism of new executive homes, the new school building is unapologetic in its distinctive presence, asking the viewer to accept that this particular school is apparently made of wood and grass, that it is triangular in shape, and that it is sitting in the middle of a field. Clearly, one must conclude, a Stealth bomber has landed in Essex.

Environmental and sustainable design

One of the great pleasures of the last twelve years has been working with the emerging practice of AHMM. I first met the four partners in late-1990, just as Atelier Ten was established. Their office was around the corner and although it was some years before we worked together on a proper project we collaborated in the strict diet of potential projects that is so often the lot of the young architectural practice, as well as in teaching at the Bartlett, where I was the environmental critic for their design unit for a brief period.

The issues surrounding environmental and sustainable design have always been a key part of the dialogue between us. Their Live-In Room 'house of glass', an unbuilt proposition (but a marvel of practice promotion), was at one level an early failure in this regard as it represented the success of the iconic over the pragmatic but, at another level, our long discussions about the issues surrounding glass and the internal environment have been replayed and refined over the years on a succession of projects. The office's cartoon of the scheme in the style of a Tintin adventure was published in the Sunday Times and attracted some attention from the guardians of Hergé's estate but also a couple of interested potential clients. I was not-so-secretly quite relieved when nothing came of the enquiries, though I am sure the result would have been an architectural tour-de-force!

At Great Notley Primary School, the whole range of sustainable issues came to the fore. The development of the scheme following the team's success in the competition was an intense and rather extraordinary voyage through the design process. Initially, we set about designing the 'model of sustainability' including courtyards, solar collectors and even a windmill, but we were brought up hard against the fact that although it was a landmark scheme there would be no additional funds available to pay for sustainability enhancements.

Work was then done in minimising plan and external wall area while retaining the idealised classroom diagrams for natural light and cross ventilation, and this led directly to the form as built. Everything was optimised against function and performance, and in particular we moved the classroom façades away from the Passive Solar Wall / Direct Gain designs that were so much a feature of the guidelines of the time and have resulted in overheated classrooms in many schools since the 1970s.

One method of work particular to AHMM is the way that they run their design development meetings. Unlike the traditional design team meeting, this takes more the form of a crit session where the latest evolution of the scheme is pinned up and described, and then everybody is involved in debate and dissection of the issues, sometimes under very direct questioning. You have to be prepared to be intuitive in responses; there is no time for detailed analysis (that comes later) but because the office is so open to comment and change these sessions frequently lead to the next step change in the evolution of the scheme.

It says a great deal for their doggedness and skill that they iterated and re-iterated their proposition for Great Notley to get it to function so effectively within such a tight budget. The building won more awards than any building ever commissioned by Essex County Council. It is a great shame that because of the vagaries of OJEC and PFI this excellent design cannot be replicated around the county, and an even greater shame that when Essex needed the school extended they got someone else to do it! "There is nothing more uncommon than common sense" (Frank Lloyd Wright)

Patrick Bellew

Project 4:2
West Pier 2000

Date
1987–88

Location
Exhibited in Brighton,
Brisbane and London

Client
Building Design
British Steel

> **Context and comment**

> The winning entry for a Building Design and UIA competition to develop Brighton's famous West Pier, first constructed in 1866 by Eugenius Birch and later declared unsafe in 1975.

> The new design restores Birch's original pierhouse and deck, and extends it one kilometre out to sea, this projection being punctuated by various architectural events. The intention is to reject the typical current manifestation of piers as self-contained buildings or plazas on stilts, and instead to return to the original concept of the pier as a place of experience and encounter.

> Central to West Pier 2000 is a proposition about what mechanisms have to do in order to make an architectural thing, rather than what a pier should look like.

> The partial collapse of West Pier during stormy weather and a fire in early 2003 suggests that, perhaps, the new scheme's time has come.

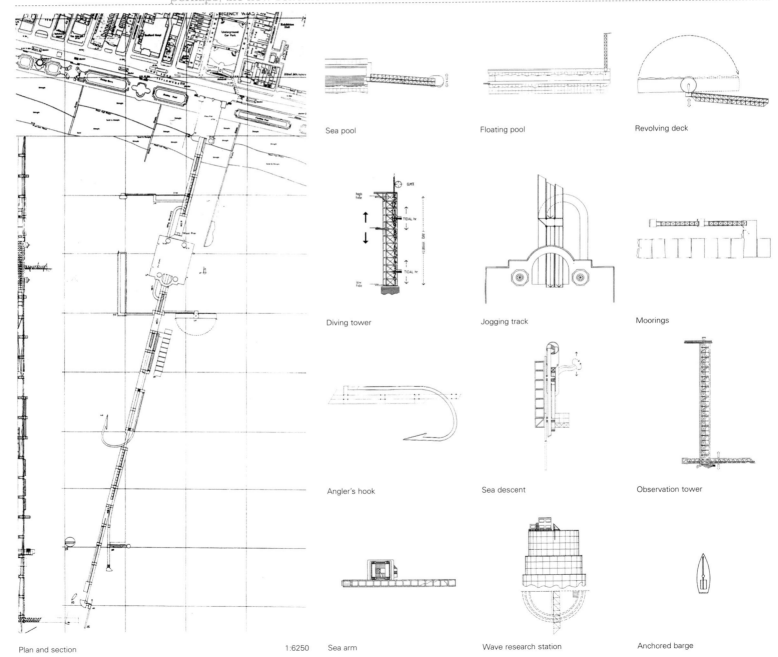

Sea pool

Floating pool

Revolving deck

Diving tower

Jogging track

Moorings

Angler's hook

Sea descent

Observation tower

Plan and section   1:6250   Sea arm

Wave research station

Anchored barge

4:2.1 Sun

A revolving deck provides a perfectly aligned platform for sun-bathing. As the human body is synchronised with the solar movement across the sky, the shadow of the anchor pile indicates to each sun-bather their optimum orientation towards the sun.

A floating pool offers similar opportunities for sunning, this time within the quiet confines of two buoyant concrete walls separated by steel grillage. The latter allows small fish and waves to pass within, adding to an overall atmosphere of contemplation and the tension between sun, sky, sea and horizon.

In the observation tower, stairs climb some 100m to provide stunning panoramic views. On clear days, these vistas reach right over to France.

4:2.2 Sea

The diving tower moves up and down some 13 storeys in response to tidal movements. The relative slowness of this oscillation is in marked contrast to the sudden bodily release and plummet of successive divers as they launch themselves into the sea below.

The sea pool, anchored onto the sea bed, is always flooded with sea water and remains calm internally. Its relation to the sea is, however, dramatically controlled through its ramp-and-buoy element, which acts as valve in order to reverse within the pool the actions of tidal movement.

A range of moorings allows for the continual shuttling of visiting boats and pleasure craft. This is one of the most bustling parts of the pier.

The 'sea descent' allows inspection of the submarine world of the sea. A marine laboratory and sub-aqua club are cantilevered off a steel sea wall, while a lift and stairs provide access to a diving bell. In a similarly inquisitive mode, the wave research station positioned off the western side of the main pier examines the power of the sea and our potential to understand and harness it. Suspended from the observation tower, the 'sea arm' moves vertically in correspondence with the tides. It is periodically washed over by occasional waves.

4:2.3 Wind

A jogging track allows for more energetic bodily movement, the runner's body being invigorated by the air swirling around it in complementary cycles of movement.

The 'angler's hook' provides a more contemplative exposure to the wind, this time the calm peace of walking, casting and waiting being given an exposed platform on which to take place. Time passes slowly here.

The anchored barge provides stasis, with movement being possible only when the two screw piles are retracted and repositioned. Away from the main pier, the wind here is much stronger.

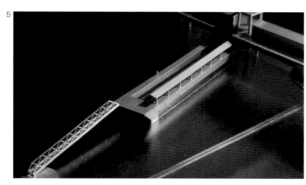

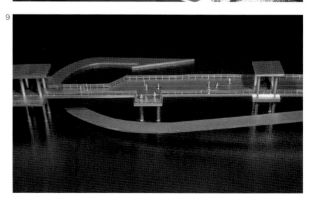

Project 4:3 Monsoon	**> Context and comment** > A c. £11 million refurbishment of an existing office and depot as the new office headquarters for a fashionable retail company.
Date 2000	> The building was originally designed by Paul Hamilton of Bicknall & Hamilton as the road-transport interface of the rail-freight operation in nearby Paddington station. Completed in 1969 at the same time as London's Westway (a freeway-style elevated road), the depot physically intersects with the Westway and is seemingly carved out of the same massive quantities of cheap concrete. The building is divided into two parts – a large 'battleship' main building for workshops, offices, loading bays and canteens, and a smaller rotunda for vehicle storage. It is Grade II* listed as a building of historic architectural importance.
Location Paddington, London	
Client Monsoon Plc	> Despite evident architectural quality, the depot was abandoned and fell into disrepair during the 1990s. To prevent further decay, and to circumnavigate labyrinthine ownership and planning complications, property adviser David Rosen recognised the opportunity for a speedy refurbishment, ready for occupation as the HQ of the high-street fashion store Monsoon
	> The architectural process proceeded at a rapid pace, work beginning on site effectively without formal planning permission, watched by a prestigious client, Westminster City Council, English Heritage and the Twentieth Century Society.
	> The design response deals with layers of fabric and temporality, choosing where to intervene and where not to, and interweaving the past, present and future into a newly recharged piece of architecture.

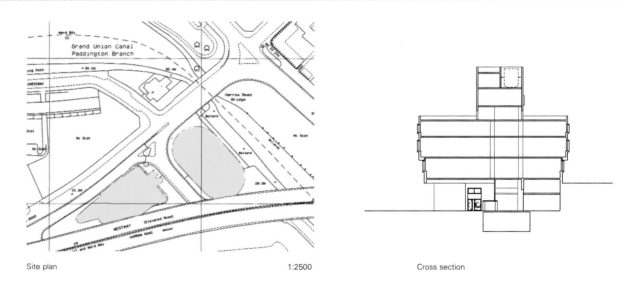

Site plan   1:2500   Cross section

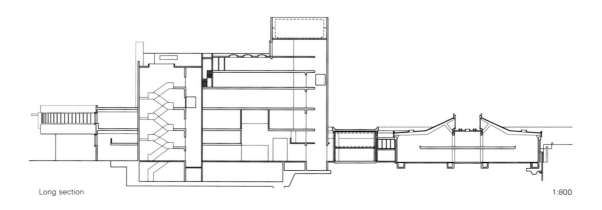

Long section   1:800

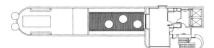

Fifth floor plan

Sixth floor plan

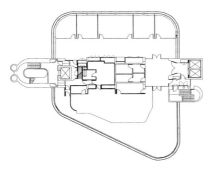

Third floor plan

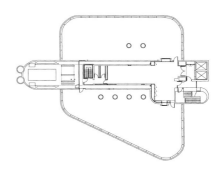

Fourth floor plan

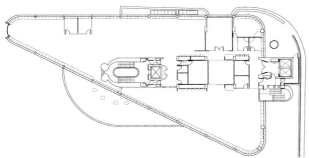

First floor plan

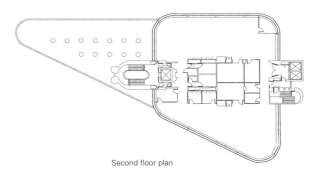

Second floor plan

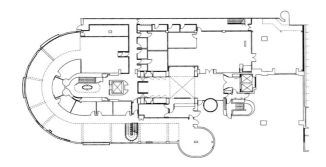

Ground floor plan

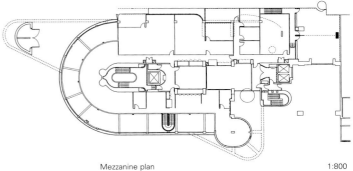

Mezzanine plan

1:800

Fig 1 Original publication of building in 1969

Fig 2 View from west in 1969

Fig 3 Rotunda in 1969

Fig 4 Proposal for entrance

Fig 5 Proposal for access area beneath the Westway

Opposite: Refurbished internal staircase

4:3.1 Strategies of time

The original building possessed undeniable presence born out of highly mannered form, eccentric urban positioning and monumental materiality. The strategy at Monsoon has been to rework the enormity of the structure with the overall result that it almost looks as if no architect has been there at all. In fact, ghostly architectural presence/absence is revealed by a myriad of different professional tactics, from alterations of volume and structure to details of surface and fit-out. What holds this all together is a strategy of temporality as much as of space – a strategy which seeks to animate the building into a multiplicity of remembered pasts, known presents and possible futures.

4:3.2 Past I: battleship

The first engagement with the past is to take existing architectural elements of the main battleship building and either to restore them to an acceptable condition, and/or to reuse them in a more appropriate way. Hence the sandblasting of the original 60s mosaics, the refurbishment of the existing stairs and the reworking of the goods lift into two high-quality passenger elevators. New double- and secondary-glazed windows have been added to Hamilton's ribbon strips, while preserving the extant fenestration grid and pattern. The mosaics have been repaired using the same Japanese supplier from 30 years ago. And, of course, there has been an intensive cleansing regime for the whole project, getting deep into the pores of the concrete.

4:3.3 Past II: rotunda

For the smaller rotunda building, the office reinstated the shell of the architecture, and in doing so an additional and unique condition was revealed. During the years when it had been abandoned by its official owners, this structure was appropriated for a series of illegal concerts, ephemeral art installations and other experimental events – the post-industrial noise and art performance group Test Department were one of those to exploit the space. Today, the only lasting traces of such activities are a series of graffiti sprayings, manifestations of a particularly nihilist movement that is highly valued within this specific subcultural genre. Now that the rotunda space has been turned into the HQ of Nissan's European car-styling department, these pieces of graffiti, with the help of English Heritage, have been preserved under a layer of protective plasterboard, awaiting inspection by future generations of cultural historians, anthropologists and archaeologists.

4:3.4 Present-future I: operation

Despite the manifest advantages of the original structure, the Monsoon building has required serious reworking before it can operate properly within the context of twenty-first century codes and expectations. A front door – missing from the 1969 configuration – has been added for pedestrians. Chill beam air conditioning, along with cabling and lighting, nestles into the structure, thus obviating the need for either suspended ceilings or messily exposed services. A new triple-height reception has been hewn out of the concrete by cutting through existing floors, and three floors of former plant have been reclaimed for office use – a total 15,000 square feet has been added to the useable floorplate.

4:3.5 Present-future II: arts

Apart from Monsoon's primary future as an office headquarters, the scheme also encompasses other, more unusual operations. Peter Simon, the majority owner of Monsoon, has hung his personal collection of contemporary art from developing countries on the building's internal walls. The office also designed a large glass box – effectively a gigantic vitrine – to display a piece by the South Korean artist Soo-Ja Kim entitled *Cities on the Move: Bottari Truck* which consists of a yellow flat-bed truck laden with brightly-coloured fabrics.

In a somewhat different manifestation of its changing life, post-configuration Monsoon, with its newly extended fenestration and late-evening working patterns, projects its internal activities across the Westway. This is especially apparent at night, when the flashing headlights of passing motorists on the adjacent high-level road are countered by the highly-proximate illuminated strips of the building's linear windows.

Both conditions present a uniquely attenuated aesthetic condition – one as fine art fabricated from canvas and oil, the other as quotidian art composed from everyday journeys and work.

Fig 6 Interior undergoing refurbishment

Fig 7 New mezzanine floor

Fig 8 *Cities on the Move: Bottari Truck*. Still from video by Soo-Ja Kim

Fig 9 Refurbished staircase

Fig 10 Grafitti in rotunda

Fig 11 View from west after refurbishment

Fig 12 Exterior and interior after refurbishment

Opposite:
View from below Westway, after refurbishment

Project 4:4	> **Context and comment**
Union Square	> Urban redevelopment containing office, housing and retail facilities.
Date	> An exercise in urban as much as architectural design, extending the 'Bankside triangle'-focused
2002	regeneration of Southwark further south. Union Square creates a new counterpoint to the
	Tate Modern, Millennium Bridge, Globe Theatre and Thames Path to its immediate north.
Location	
Southwark	> By exploiting a gap site backing onto railway land, four distinct blocks create 120,000 ft²
	of residences, retail, office and commercial floorspace, as well as forming a new public square.
Client	
Lake Estates	> Prepared in conjunction with Roger Zogolovitch and Lake Estates as developer, and
Dorrington Estates	MBM Arquitectes of Barcelona for urban design guidelines.

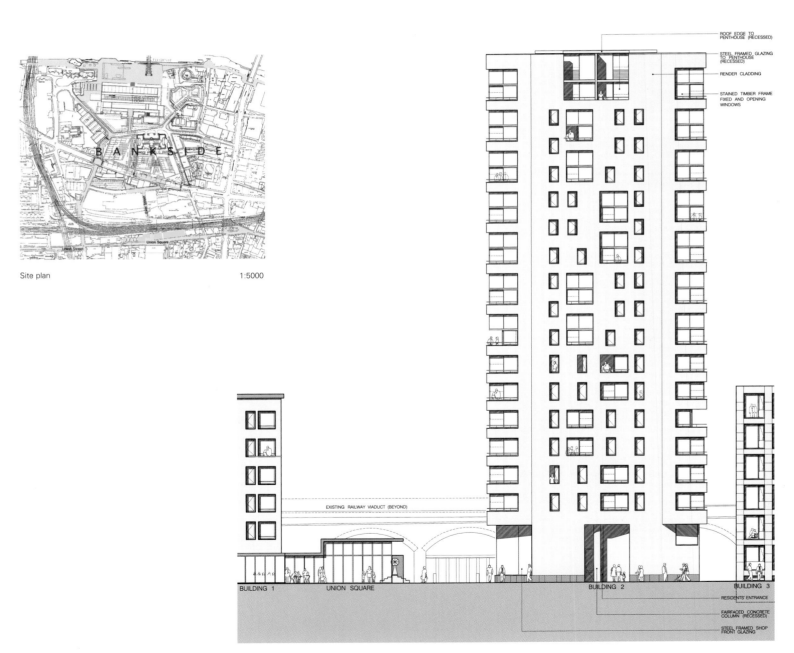

Site plan   1:5000

South elevation   1:400

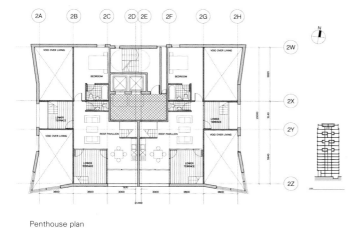

Penthouse plan

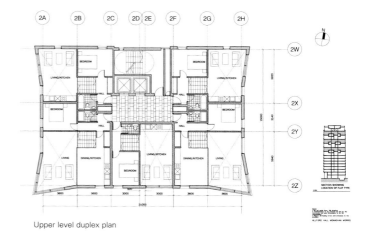

Upper level duplex plan

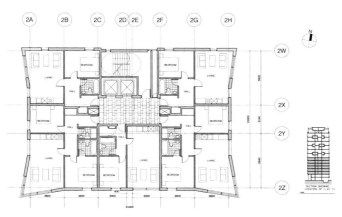

Typical floor plan

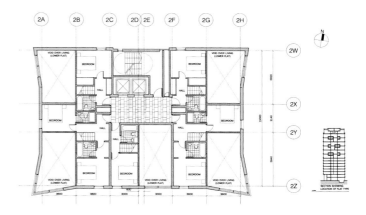

Entry level duplex plan

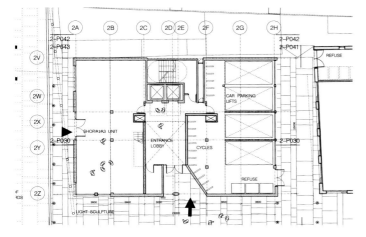

Ground floor plan

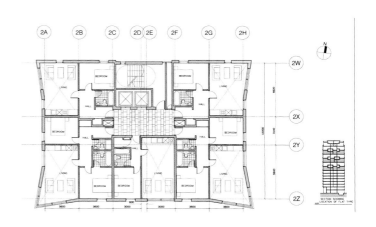

1¹/₂ height apartment plan

1:400

4:4.1 Silhouette

Much is written and spoken about the London skyline, a great deal of it overly concerned with the protection of views of St Paul's cathedral (immediately to the north of Union Square) and other churches. Determined to respond to a more local and variegated skyline, the office conducted an analysis of elevation to both the north and south of Union Street, demonstrating an immense variation in both height and typology, while also underlining the importance of interconnectivity with important sites all around the scheme. This analysis helped inform the new silhouette of Union Square which stresses undulation and variation rather than constancy and uniformity.

4:4.2 Breaking up the block

Rather than imposing a single, large block, the urban design of Union Square finds its architectural resolution in the form of four distinct blocks or 'tall houses', each adding its own unique architecture to the site while also contributing to the composition of the whole.

For example, the tallest block, containing market-rate apartments, is slightly splayed at each corner, creating a subtle modification to its architectural neighbour across Ewer Street, a lower residential block containing affordable units for key workers. To the east, two office and commercial buildings share a common service core, but offer variable heights and volumetric compositions. The effect is of a family of architectures, expressing individual qualities and characters within an overall unifying composition.

4:4.3 Firming up the square

Between the four 'tall houses' sits Union Square, a new space opened up by the development and connecting, via Ewer Street, under the railway lines and up towards Tate Modern. By implementing traffic calming and hard landscaping, this new public space is then further extended southward, right across Union Street.

A larger space – both in a psychological and a physical sense – is thus opened up, emphasising the importance of public space to the development. Union Square now becomes a key moment in the scheme, a calm and reflective zone, enlivened by bordering cafés and restaurants, in what was previously only a wide and ugly traffic thoroughfare.

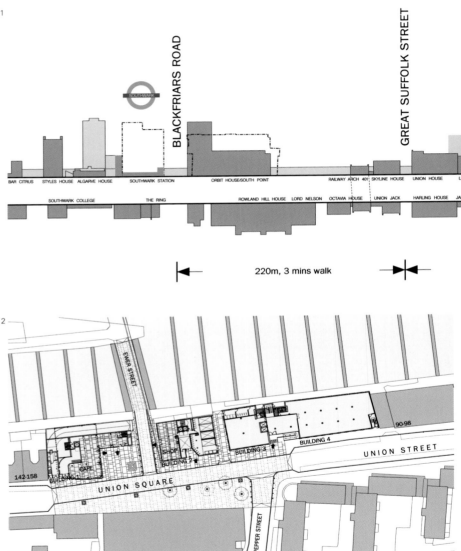

Fig 1 Union Street: analysis of scale

Fig 2 Site plan

Fig 3 View from south across
       Union Square

Fig 4 Southwark from the air

Fig 5 Bankside context

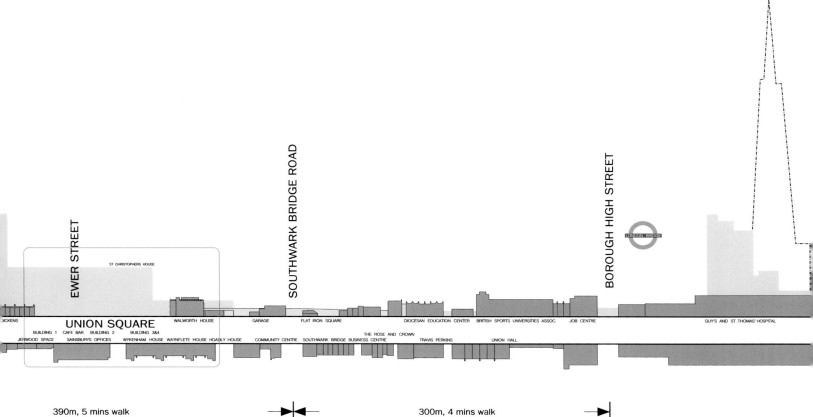

EWER STREET

SOUTHWARK BRIDGE ROAD

BOROUGH HIGH STREET

LONDON BRIDGE

DICKENS

ST CHRISTOPHERS HOUSE

UNION SQUARE

WALWORTH HOUSE

GARAGE

FLAT IRON SQUARE

DIOCESAN EDUCATION CENTER

BRITISH SPORTS UNIVERSITIES ASSOC.

JOB CENTRE

GUY'S AND ST. THOMAS' HOSPITAL

BUILDING 1 CAFE BAR BUILDING 2 BUILDING 3&4

THE ROSE AND CROWN

JERWOOD SPACE SAINSBURYS OFFICES WYKENHAM HOUSE WAYNFLETE HOUSE HOADLY HOUSE COMMUNITY CENTRE SOUTHWARK BRIDGE BUSINESS CENTRE TRAVIS PERKINS UNION HALL

390m, 5 mins walk

300m, 4 mins walk

4

5 Bankside: The Strategy

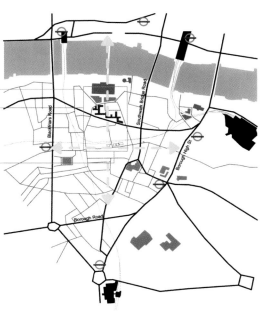

Tate Modern south side entrance

Redevelopment of St Christopher House

Union Square and street improvements

Bankside area benefits from the transport linkages by tube, overland rail, bus, and river. Numerous projects on the Thames Path have created a vibrant east-west pedestrian route along the river. The extension of this integrated public space network both north-south and east-west, through the middle and lower Bankside area has yet to be realised.

The Bankside Urban Study by Richard Rogers Partnership (completed earlier this year) identifies the links with key nodes in the area; the Tate Modern and riverside, Borough Market, Borough Station, Elephant and Castle and, Southwark Station benefit those living, working and visiting the Bankside area.
The report puts forward a recommended strategic agenda to:

strengthen and create linkages and a resource of open spaces

enhance the public realm and streetscape

reinforce neighbourhood identity

We believe that the proposed Union Square project meets all the aspirations of the plan and provides a stepping stone in building these links to north-south and east-west connections.

Strategy Plan 1:5000

Project 4:5
New Garden House

Date
2002

Location
Hatton Garden, London

Client
Derwent Valley
Properties

> **Context and comment**
> A dense urban site with frontage on to London's Hatton Garden, famous for its diamond shops and merchants.

> The existing building on to Hatton Garden dates from the 1930s, but was extensively and unsympathetically refurbished in the 1970s, including major revisions to the main façade.

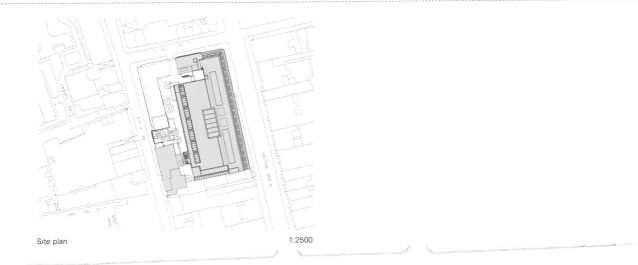

Site plan   1:2500

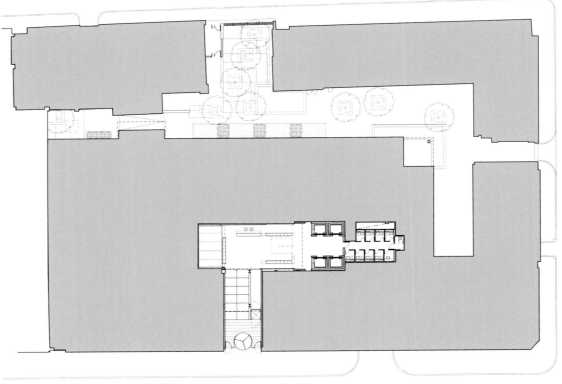

Ground plan   1:500

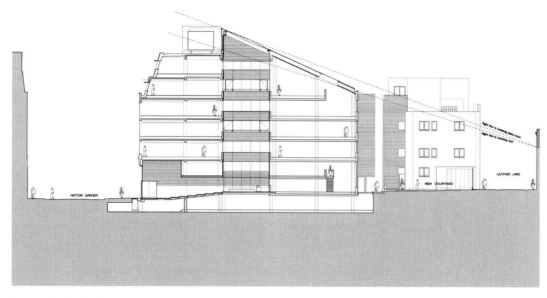

Cross section through atrium

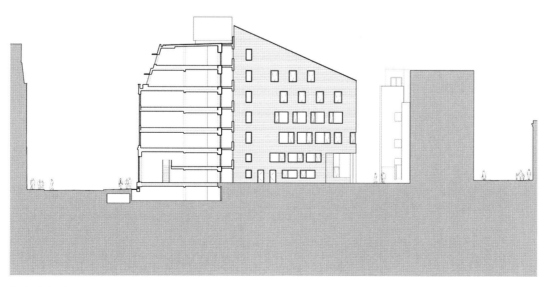

Sectional elevation

1:500

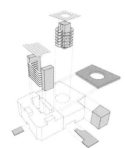

4:5.1 Dock

At Morelands, the office worked hard to maintain the grain of the existing back-lot. At New Garden House, working for the same developer, Wilmar/Derwent Valley, but now on a much larger and more prestigious site, a far more ambitious strategy is adopted. Within the large open courtyard a whole new building is inserted, slim German bricks in two colour tones rendering it quite distinct from its architectural neighbours.

New Garden House thus appears in the manner of a ship docking, its impressive bulk leaning against the harbour sides, with vertical slots of space driven down between ship and wharf. Bridging across is a new atrium which provides the visitor, once inside, with a homogeneous and unified interior.

4:5.2 Landing stage

Key to New Garden House is its atrium, a central reception pinned deep in the heart of the newly reconfigured structure, and reached through a stepped entrance from Hatton Garden. Inside, the visitor is presented with architecture of a grand order: a five-storey atrium containing a mezzanine lobby and flooded with light from the EFTE roof above. From here, the rest of the building is immediately accessible.

Fig 1 Atrium study

Fig 2 Spatial interventions at Centric House – another refurbishment project for Derwent Valley

Fig 3 Entrance study

Fig 4 Courtyard elevation detail

Opposite: Atrium, sectional perspective

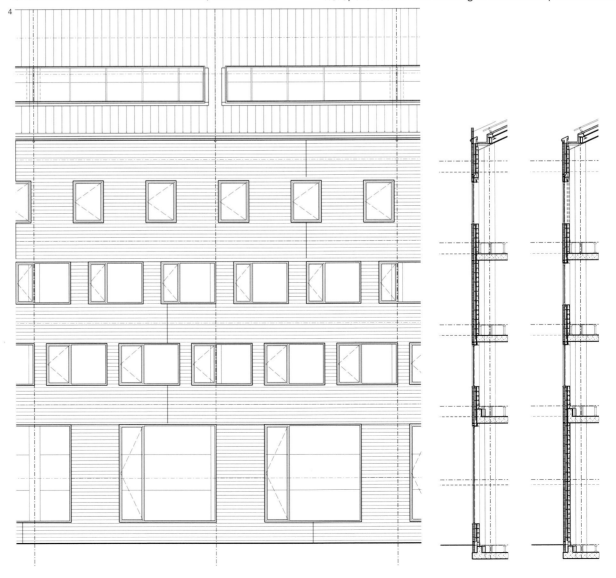

Project 4:6	**> Context and comment**
Poolhouse	> Stand-alone building containing an enclosed pool area and additional guest accommodation.
Date	> Constructed for Simon Allford's parents Beryl and David in the garden of their Wiltshire home.
1990–94	David Allford, himself a well-known architect, took a keen interest in the design development.
Location	> The office's first opportunity to undertake a building with four elevations led to an enormous
Wiltshire	amount of architectural invention and effort being packed into a compact construction. The
	result, perhaps surprisingly for such an early and self-evidently manifesto project, is neither
Client	overly complex nor boastful.
Beryl and David Allford	
	> Understanding the Poolhouse necessitates an appreciation of the way in which it at once
	counters and defers to the surrounding landscape – physically, visually and mentally.

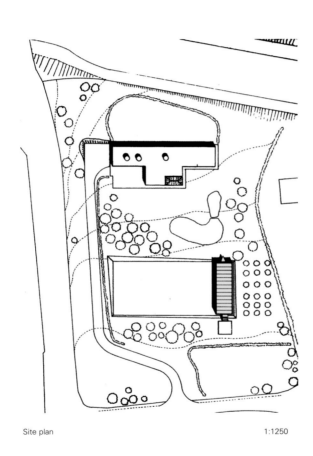

Site plan   1:1250

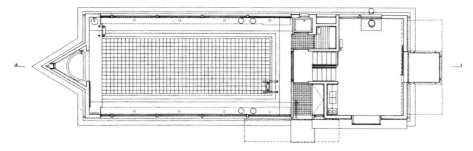

Ground floor plan

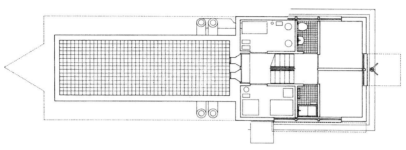

Upper floor plan

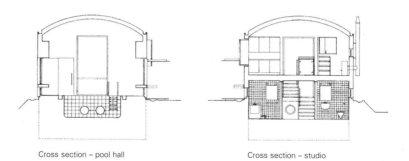

Cross section – pool hall

Cross section – studio

Long section

1:200

4:6.1 A guest in the garden

The Poolhouse – which in addition to its pool, contains a guest apartment and additional sleeping quarters – sits well away from the main house, adopting the manner of a guest in the garden, undoubtedly present while always respectfully discrete. The relation between architecture and landscape is at first presented as one of detachment, where the pool remains forever apart both from the garden outside (there are no opening windows or screens) and the guest apartment (separated from the pool by a kind of interstitial airlock).

Similarly, the self-containment of the rectangular profile is preserved by a low-level moat-like drainage channel which tracks the building footprint, and by the absence of all but the most necessary of entrances and access points.

4:6.2 Elemental relations

Despite the apparent separation of architecture and garden, the Poolhouse does indeed reconnect with its surroundings. A series of different windows and views offer visual engagements of fluctuating condition and energy: the horizontal window at the base of the pool hall provides momentary glimpses of the garden whose exact nature are determined by the rhythm and speed of the swimmer; the immovable full height glass screen between pool hall and guest apartment sets up a contrast between physical separation and visual connectivity; peepholes and portholes tempt naughty glances at bodies in the bedrooms and below the pool surface. And most intriguingly, a square window in the living area – created to satisfy the demands of Beryl Allford that she can watch sunsets – articulates a highly mannered architectural expression of vision, the metal-framed window being punched outward from the cedar building skin in order to stress the special nature of the viewing act.

Through such visual and architectural devices, the Poolhouse circumvents its own seeming physical aloofness; architecture and landscape are ultimately not unconnected at all, rather they are conjoined by oppositional relation and differential visual condition. For the inhabitant, whether swimmer or guest, what might have been a place of seclusion becomes far more, a kind of machine by which to view the garden beyond, and hence to provoke thoughts and contemplation far in excess of a purely internalised private world.

The Old Man

David Allford, Simon's father, occupies a special place in the history of AHMM. From providing sophisticated architectural input to his son at an early age, David quickly entered into the lives of the other partners in subtle and persuasive ways: as consultant and joke-teller, as client and confidant, and as sage and raconteur, offering everything from accurate advice and inspirational motivation to scurrilous gossip and well-timed warnings.

Talking to the four partners, they recall many moments when, faced with a particular crisis or problem, Simon would report back from a conversation with 'the old man'; advice and support would thus filter back into the office on such matters as design sophistication, the recession or the loss of a competition.

It was David who set up the impressive list of consultants for the Fifth Man diploma project. It was David who, with his wife Beryl, provided the office's first new build commission. And it was David who provided design crits as well as far too many late night meals, drinks and architectural conversations. In all of this, he was never anything but outspoken, yet importantly his language was always plain and simple; David never had any time for the mystification of architecture even though intellectually he could run rings round most of its more theoretically minded exponents. The phrase the partners continue to enjoy most is one David learned from an earlier associate, his oft-repeated, half-mocking, half-serious description of modernism as 'flat roofs and bags of glass.'

A life-long supporter of Sheffield Wednesday, a recounter of stories and relayer of architectural gossip, he was a man who would always chat to you, never mind who else more important might be in the room. David died in 1997.

Iain Borden

Fig 1 Queen Victoria's bathing hut, Isle of Wight

Fig 2 Barn in Wiltshire

Fig 3 Square window, east side

Fig 4 The swimmer's view

Fig 5 Pool with view through to studio

Opposite: View from south-east

Overleaf: West elevation

5:0 Interacting

Traditionally, at the centre of much architectural ideology lies the notion that the architect is an autonomous figure, an artist with almost complete control over the architecture which they produce. Most extreme in this view of things is the hyper-individualist figure of Howard Roark, the Architect-Superman at the centre of Ayn Rand's novel The Fountainhead, the architect who believes that he and he alone is the sole true creator and owner of his architectural designs. In Rand's novel (later a Hollywood film with Gary Cooper cast as Roark) this argument is used to legitimise Roark's right personally to dynamite a housing estate which had been built without due attention to his original instructions.

Of course, such dramatic – and in this case fictional – events are but a grossly distorted parody of the real processes of architectural design, construction and operation, wherein a multitude of different peoples of different professions, expertise and knowledge come together to create architecture. Much recent thinking and research recognises this, explicitly seeking to promote new ways of working and communicating in the construction industry as a whole.

The challenge for the architect is not then how to dominate or belittle other voices and energies, but how to work with them, to encourage them and to gain the best possible building out of that interaction. The AHMM office, like other practices, has chosen exactly this route in many if not all of their projects, setting up either special one-off, or continuing and close working relationships with, among others, artists, graphic designers, structural engineers, environmental consultants, landscape designers, planners, furniture and product designers, academics, members of the public and builders. Similarly, within the domain of architecture itself they have equivalent relationships with other architects, with students and, not least, with each other. This chapter sets out some of these relationships – not all are necessarily about highly collaborative work, and indeed more than one is about resolution through confrontation, but they all bear witness to the realisation that all architects do indeed interact with others, and that interaction must be recognised and faced up to, if good architecture is to result.

Project 5:1	> Context and comment
Designing for Doctors	> Exhibition on contemporary surgery design.

Date
1993

> In the 1990s, the Tomlinson Report criticised health care in London for spending too much on hospitals and too little on the facilities of local doctors and health centres. £130 million was therefore made available to assist London doctors' surgeries with new buildings and improvements.

Location
RIBA and British
Medical Association

> The British Medical Association (BMA) approached the RIBA to create an exhibition on architectural work in the healthcare field.

Client
RIBA and British
Medical Association

> AHMM consequently worked with the BMA, RIBA and the Family Health Service Authority (FHSA) of the London Borough of Camden & Islington on the "Designing for Doctors" exhibition – promoting both the opportunity for medical work to architects and, conversely, the benefits of good architecture to medical clients.

Fig 1 Exhibition catalogue, cover

Fig 2 Exhibition catalogue,
page spread

5:1.1 Architecture for architects
Like the *Under 50K* exhibition (Refer to *Getting Things Done/ Under 50K*), one of the main forms of interaction was with the numerous other architects who contributed to the show. Every practice had to provide their own materials at their own expense, ready to fit into a predetermined format designed by AHMM with Studio Myerscough. Each was essentially pitching for its own share of the burgeoning healthcare market.

Fig 1 Internal courtyard ramp

Fig 2 Internal courtyard

5:2.1 Research and development

In order to meet the Joseph Rowntree Foundation's demand for stringent control over costs, and hence to keep eventual rental levels as low as possible, it was essential that the architect work in extremely close collaboration with the builder. Although the initial contractor withdrew after the design competition had been won, the practice tendered out for another contractor at their own initiative and cost. Sisk were selected, and, despite initial doubts on the part of Rowntree, a complex series of contracts and agreements were quickly drawn up between client, architect and contractor; the financial risk for the project was ultimately borne by Sisk.

There followed three months of intensive work with Sisk to lower costs down from £2.6 to £2.1 million. Every single component was thoroughly researched in order to identify cheaper and better alternatives, factories were visited and questioned, the structural engineers Adams Kara Taylor produced elegant bridges at minimal cost, while modular bathrooms were adopted to reduce build times. The use of a long internal ramp down the middle of the scheme (a suggestion from Sisk) reduced soil movement costs by connecting the grade level front entrance with the higher rear level of the building.

5:2.2 Partnering and M4I

Behind all this lies a number of different driving forces within the construction industry. Firstly, this is exactly the sort of 'Partnering' project proposed by John Egan in the Construction Task Force's *Rethinking Construction* report (1996), itself the follow-up to Michael Latham's *Constructing the Team* report (1994). Both reports urge architect and contractor to work together not in a confrontational manner but in a collaborative team seeking common goals and profits.

Secondly, it also responds to the 'Movement for Innovation' (M4I) initiative, which represents the most practical side of the Egan report. In M4I, an assessment of the project is made to identify new ways of working, from procurement to production, with eventual benefits seen as improved value for money for clients, more profits for the architects, the suppliers and contractors, and better products for end users. M4I speaks the language of customer satisfaction, of value maximisation over cost minimisation, and, at CASPAR at least, it works, producing affordable homes of a size and quality unobtainable elsewhere in the private sector rental market.

| Project 5:3 | > **Context and comment** |
| MoMo Apartments | > Research project for a relocatable system of mass-housing. |

Date
2002

> Exploits lessons learned at Raines Dairy and similar schemes, with additional input from Cedric Price acting as consultant.

Location
Various

> Aimed at temporarily available sites with varying time periods, such as disused railways, land earmarked for future development or even floating platforms. At the end of the site's availability, the whole structure will be demounted and moved elsewhere.

Client
Peabody Trust

> Intended to house residents on the move, such as those on the homeless list, those awaiting permanent housing, tenants decanted from estates being refurbished, etc.

> The most likely clients will be local authorities, many of whom are already spending large sums of money on 'bed & breakfast' and other temporary accommodation. If the local authorities provide the land, Peabody will then provide the MoMo apartments and lease them back to the municipality on a non-profit basis.

> However temporary the housing, the units are designed to support and engender a notion of 'home'.

> MoMo = Mobile Modular

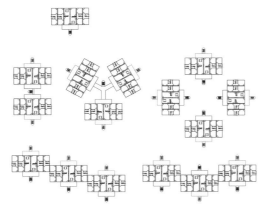

Possible configurations   1:2500

Living/dining unit   2-bedroom unit   2 x 1-bedroom unit
Type A   Type B   Type C   1:200

Perspective view of linear configuration

Fig 1 WH Davis
publicity material

Fig 2 Airstream
caravan

Fig 3 Bedroom

Fig 4 Kitchen

Fig 5 Living room

5:3.1 Technology transfer

Peabody housing designed by the office at Raines Dairy naturally lead to notions of prefabrication, serial production and industrialised construction. For MoMo, however, rather than continuing to collaborate solely with the existing manufacturers of industrialised architecture the office chose to explore interaction with three very different kinds of producer: WH Davis, manufacturers of transport containers and equipment; Tilden Industries, manufacturers of industrialised architecture on a project-by-project basis; and Hansen T.I.S, prefabricators of architectural units. These variable areas of manufacture offer the promise of real technology transfer, untapping sources of expertise and technology as yet unknown to the architectural world.

5:3.2 Flexible specification

These producers are not, of course, to be allowed to design and produce whatever they see fit. Instead, the office has drawn up a very carefully prescribed yet flexible set of specifications for such elements as the module floor structure, roof structure, roof panel, floor areas, performance criteria, and minimum/maximum overall dimensions.

By such means, MoMo remains open to suggestions of alternative materials, systems and sizes as might suit the best-value provider and without compromising design ideals. Later discussions with manufacturers will then lead to design refinement, using the most appropriate technology to achieve the best standard product at the most economic cost.

5:3.4 Fit-out and finish

Borrowing from the idea of a holiday, the interior fit-out adopts the persona of a seaside hut or caravan: minimal space, but fully-fitted and serviced, and with the capacity for individual personalisation. Flexible internal plans and robust finishes such as cork flooring and wooden walls are accompanied by adjustable wardrobes (alterable into desk or sleeping accommodation as required), kitchens configurable with island units or dining table, sliding windows with full-height glazing, clothing and storage hooks, and the provision for the display of pictures and ornaments.

While by no means 'luxury' housing, by such measures MoMo offers an interstitial stage between being homeless and being at home. MoMo is a provisional home, giving relief from the alienation of displacement and constant migration.

5:3.3 Touch the ground lightly

The office are now working on how to service the temporary sites for MoMo. For example, although these are relatively light buildings, they still need foundations; so a collaboration with Happolds is looking at different options, including one possible solution involving manually-jacked up railway sleepers. A 'skirt' around the building supplies electricity and water at ground-level, while a cess-pit (emptied at frequent intervals) deals with sewage and waste.

5:3.5 Spacing time

Notions of time are central to MoMo, offering respite to those who have either been uprooted or estranged. By using land that is temporarily unused (such as that awaiting development), and by providing reconfigurable and relocatable housing, MoMo offers architectural insertion into the city that is unique in its exploitation of hitherto unrealised time-space assets. MoMo is not permanent architecture, but it could become a permanent and much-needed new feature of urban development.

Project 5:4
The Fifth Man

Date
1985–86

Location
The Bartlett, UCL

> Context and comment
> The final prize-winning diploma project undertaken by the AHMM partners when they were all at The Bartlett, UCL, and submitted in the summer of 1986.

> The four individuals opted to produce not separate portfolios but a collective project which investigated the development of commercial office space in four buildings on the Little Britain site in the City of London. Working systematically through a series of discrete stages, moving from the abstract and generic to the specific and particular, the final collaborative portfolio – The Fifth Man – represents at once a team, a product, an architecture and a way of working.

> The only time when the partners have ever tried to write (as opposed to design) together, what the quartet said then still holds for the office now: the necessity of understanding issues of site, space, finance, technology, architectural typology and the whole mechanism of the city if new architecture.

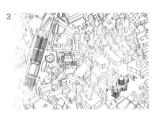

Fig 1–4 Extracts from
The Fifth Man

Fig 5 *The Fifth Man* cover

''The Fifth Man project is predicated on twin beliefs.

First, that it is in the field of everyday building rather than public building that modern architecture has failed the city.

We began the programme by investigating opportunities for building both within and on the periphery of the City of London. Our objective was to create an urban stage with a space and four buildings. Once a site had been selected a programme for architecture was generated by responses to the architectural and urban context

The functional programme was determined by the location of the chosen site: financial logic demands that the everyday buildings in the City of London are speculative offices and we accepted this programme.

No rules or theories of architecture were established. The site plan, the individual buildings and the collective character they create were developed through the technique of collaging drawings together at regular intervals and criticising each stage as we confronted it.''

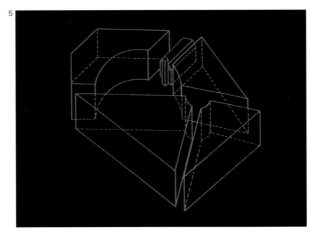

5:4.1 The Fifth Member

If the quartet of Simon, Jonathan, Peter and Paul have sometimes been compared to a rock group, then one version of the Fifth Man scenario is that there is also an actual fifth member of the band. And there is no shortage of contenders for this role. David Dunster was the Bartlett lecturer who explicitly steered the foursome in their diploma year away from working with David Chipperfield towards the tutorship of Jon Corpe. Corpe himself was the diploma tutor whose combative and abrasive style forced the students to generate self-criticism, becoming honest with their own weaknesses, and dealing with all problems with a sense of humour and irony. It was Corpe's idea that the four students should seek post-Diploma employment as a quartet, and hence perhaps lead directly to the formation of Allford Hall Monaghan Morris a few years later.

In order to complete the technical aspects of the project as quickly as possible, and in a manner which deliberately mimicked professional architectural practice, various experts were consulted during the Fifth Man process, all of whom provided important information and professional advice: Frank Duffy of DEGW and Peter Foggo of Arup Associates on the development of a new office typology, Frank Newby for structural engineering, Bill Southwood, Sam Shemmie and Ian Lyall of Ove Arup & Partners for telecommunications and services engineering, Brian Hardcastle of YRM Architects and Planners for economics and finance, and John Frazer of Fitzroy Robinson Partnership for planning and commercial constraints. And there were a myriad of other individuals: Bryn Dyer, the fellow student who began working with the other four on their collective portfolio but who chose to drop out, or Tony Martin, who allowed the four students to run up an enormous bill at his reprographics firm Sarkpoint and then refused payment (AHMM eventually forced Tony to accept £800, paid as cash in an envelope placed directly into his hand), or William Jack, the BDP boss who was amused and interested enough to actually employ all four students together.

Fig 6 Existing Little Britain site

Fig 7 Site sub-division into development plots

Fig 8 *The Generic City*

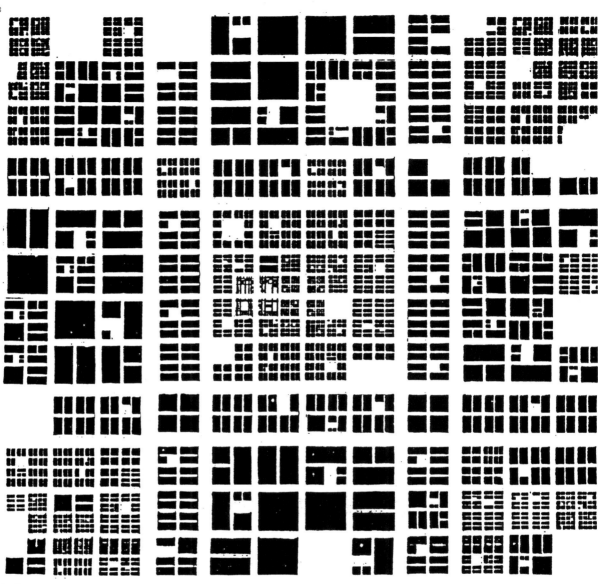

In later years, the strongest candidate for this role is, however, not one person but a collective: the AHMM office. Some of the people here have been with the practice for nearly a decade. Yet however important the individual character of any one person might be, the overall spirit and camaraderie within the practice creates a kind of collective consciousness such that, ultimately AHMM is not just individuals but also an office, a way of working, a team of personnel.

5:4.2 The Fifth Space
At the heart of the Fifth Man project is the operation of architecture in the context of the city, and, more particularly, the conception that architecture is irretrievably implicated in the construction of urban space.

"The Fifth Man represents a notion of space. In our experiment it is not simply the notion of 'four buildings – one space' but rather, as we have come to realise, the totality of the urban public realm. The explicit nature of 'The Fifth Man structure sets up the possibility of experiment at any scale."

Hence the initial explorations within the Fifth Man into The Generic City, where an entire urban composition is created out of a series of smaller and larger urban blocks themselves dependent on a series of typologies and morphologies.

The Generic City is a key image for the office, one to which the partners continue to make reference, but perhaps equally important is their realisation that it is not just the most socially worthy (housing), publicly noticeable (museums, art galleries) or unusual (the insect surgery for a butterfly collector) projects which make up architecture in the city. Rather, it is everyday buildings which constitute the urban realm as most of us encounter and comprehend it for the vast majority of our lives, and, for the Fifth Man, this everyday architecture was the speculative office,

Fig 9 Typical office floor

Fig 10 Ground floor

Fig 11 Collaged perspective view

a decision dictated by the location of the site at the fringes of the financial centre of London. In the final stage of the Diploma project, the Fifth Man emerges as a spatial scenario of office blocks, interstitial space and site, not so much stitched together as an additive collection of discrete elements as a spatial strategy of typology and urbanism.

5:4.3 The Fifth Architect
Always attuned to matters of presentational style, the four students took to wearing matching attire, carefully pre-empting all possible lines of questioning with prepared answers and semi-scripted statements. The effect was to deflect potential criticism from matters of individual effort and contribution on to more substantive issues of architectural content and intention.

In keeping with this rationale, a collective drawing style was also worked out, such that it became increasingly impossible to tell who had done which drawing. In any case, it hardly mattered, as individual options to common problems, such as the masterplan for the site, were subjected to four-way criticism and reaction before a collective decision was made on how to proceed.

"The Fifth Man is a diary of a method of working; a method that allows the individual to pursue particular architectural concerns within a developing collective scenario.

The method is explicit, for at each stage decisions taken are mapped out, continually establishing the rationale of the project, and developing the critical framework upon which it operates."

In the Fifth Man, buildings were allocated to the four individuals by lot, but group drawings were prepared showing collective views by using techniques such as spliced tracing paper sheets and (this being the early days of photocopying) photocopied background sheets onto which different options could be tested. This quickly led to one of the most constant and durable of AHMM maxims: if it's not drawn it can't be discussed.

By such processes, the four students learned to be non-possessive about their own designs but absolutely possessive and obsessive about the quality of their working practice and of the architecture and urbanism being proposed. They hence discovered a version of the architect and of architecture that was distanced from themselves as individuals, but highly personal to themselves as a four-way unit of creation.

5:4.4 The Fifth Mind
Above all else, the Fifth Man produced a way of working, a way of the four students to become an embryonic Allford Hall Monaghan Morris. This 'way of working together' is, unsurprisingly, not simple, involving not only the kinds of subtle technique, explicit sequencing and downright trickery already described, but also a highly intense psychology where each of the four, when in conversation with each other, seem to converse not only with their partners as individuals but as a foursome. It is – and it is hard to resist this comparison – a rock band kind of thing, where all manner of quirks, jibes and quizzical remarks are fused within a history of being-with-other. Entering a room when the four partners are in full flow is to encounter a kind of mad fifth mind that constantly throws out weird snatches of conversation that runs from 'Spin the wheel and take a deal', to 'liver and onions' to 'Jonathan was dying, still'. On the surface, none of this makes much (if any) sense to the outsider, but what it does do is to highlight the existence of a shared memory and sense of mutual performance that can only be born out of many nights of sleepless working, out of years and years of shared experiences both good and bad. This is the ultimate product of the Fifth Man: AHMM as autonomous entity, at once a four and an extra fifth.

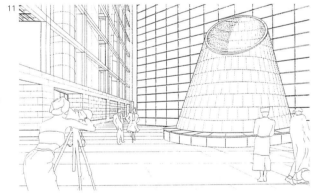

Collaborative research

Where a previous generation championed the construction of a signature style, AHMM have pioneered the renewal of interest in architecture as research and experimentation. When I joined the Bartlett, they were already about to present their 'Fifth Man' diploma project – a group effort and hence a very radical act for the 1980s. For me, they have come to embody the beginning of a new era – one of practice committed to collaborative research, developing a body of projects that are different and distinct.

Farshid Moussavi

Uncharted territory

In recent times, the study of the reciprocity of buildings begins at Purchase where Edward Larrabee-Barnes orchestrated a re-working of Jefferson's University of Virginia, with the villas designed by such luminaries as Robert Venturi, Romaldo Giurgola, Charles Gwathmey et al. – but this was a green field site. [...]

The Fifth Man, sexist perhaps, but a reference to Carol Reed's lugubrious city, explores reciprocity in what might be described as the Architecture of the gutter rather than the field. Here, the rich dense context of Little Britain forms a backdrop to a study in which the only rule controlling the reciprocity is each person's idea of architecture and the city. This idea is developed and deformed by a context that is both real and illusory, the illusory component being the group's alter-ego produced through analysis and discussion.

The density of the context precludes an extravagant tabula-rasa architecture such as the Villa Savoye or the Farnsworth House, but calls more for the architecture of Aalto's Ironworkers building in Helsinki, or Corb's own apartment block in Paris; individual, yet of the group.

The Fifth Man then is a diary of events, or better still a map of uncharted territory. It is not conclusive, but it is a record.

There is nothing so wonderful as watching people rise off the short board of received knowledge to hang ten on the wave of an idea. To record the experience reminds one of the Crystal Voyager.

Jon Corpe [Preface to 'The Fifth Man', 1986].

Project 5:5
The Office

Date
1989–present day

Location
Charlotte St (1989–1990)
Alfred Place (1990–1995)
Morelands Block A,
Old St (1995–1998)
Morelands Block B, Old
St (1998–2001)
Morelands Blocks B
and C, Old St
(2001–present day)

> **Context and comment**

> AHMM have always kept an office – not a fax-machine and a couple of Apple Macs in the backroom of a suburban house, but a real office, in the centre of town, with a proper address and real bills. Apart from instilling credibility in the eyes of clients, the office provides the partners with a psychological touchstone, a real space through which they are inescapably connected.

> The office has not been without its economic problems. When they first started up in 1989, bullish with their own success at the Bartlett and as upstart employees of BDP, Allford Hall Monaghan Morris kitted out their high-profile Charlotte Street facility with bespoke furniture and settled down to what they thought would undoubtedly be an immediately successful and prosperous career: in the first two years, they turned over £135,000 per year – not bad for a young firm. It was, however, a triumph of optimism over common sense; the recession started to hit hard in 1990, and for the next two years the office turned over just £69,000. In early 1992 they escaped the horrendously expensive rents of Charlotte Street by bluffing about a break clause in the lease. In the next office, just around the corner in Alfred Place, they fared little better; only the first rent bill was paid, and the remainder has only recently been finally paid off through small, zero interest instalments.

> In 1995 the practice moved to their current location in Clerkenwell (Refer to *Surface/Morelands*). Despite being a factor of four larger in size, the rent for the current office is no greater than that paid for Charlotte Street in the late 1980s.

> Major costs and pressures now come from other sources: for example, the AHMM printing bill for 2000 was nearly equal to their entire turnover for the year 1992. The current turnover may be well over £2 million per year but the salary bill is also over £80,000 per month.

Fig 1 1989–1990

Fig 2 1990–1995

Fig 3 1995–1998

Fig 4 1998–2001

Fig 5 2001–present day

5:5.1 Ham and High

Desperate in the early 1990s for work – any work – William Jack, their former employer at BDP, suggested that AHMM place an advert in the *Ham and High* newspaper, widely read by the intelligentsia and middle-classes of north London. Seeking to give the impression of a good, dependable local architect, just Simon Allford's name was used to represent the whole firm. A series of highly unlikely – but fee-paying – jobs promptly ensued, from a reclad bomb shelter, to planning permission for a kebab house, to a refit of the Clitterhouse Café. Strangest of all was the refurbishment of a Parker and Unwin designed house in Hampstead Garden Suburb, where the wealthy client slept on the same mattress on the floor as his 70 year-old sister, while their mother slept in a separate bed within the same room. Today, the four partners regale these stories with jokey ease, but the dark memories of such odd and downright weird times clearly still linger in the practice's collective subconscious.

5:5.2 Pocket money

In the middle of the recession, the firm's accountant – a man with a forthright attitude honed from years of advising major corporations on information resource flows and financial structures – walked in to a meeting with the partners and announced: "I know you four, you show me your magazine articles, I believe you are all alright and your buildings are interesting, but that's not my business. Let's be honest lads, basically you're insolvent and have been for the last four years. If you were anything but a partnership you would be closed down."

At this time, any fee income covered the office rent and little else. The partners paid each other whatever they needed for their individual living accommodation, plus

£30 per week cash. They all owed large amounts to the bank, varying by up to £30,000 each. As a result, when new commissions started to return in 1993, the partnership rationalised around £150,000 into what they called the 'Millennium Debt' and structured payments to erase it all by 1 January 2000 (a target which was duly achieved). Nowadays, on a Friday night the four partners still each receive a brown envelope of pocket money, as a kind of binding tradition and reminder from less fortunate times.

5:5.3 POM

When I first began working with the office on this book, and started learning rather more about the firm than could be gleaned solely from bar conversations, building visits and magazine articles, the partners took me to one side. "There is something else you should look at," they said, "Something you have to see if you want to know how we truly operate." And with that I was handed a black, A4 ring binder, not too thin and not too thick, with three small initials scribbled on the side: POM.

POM, it turns out, stands for Project Operation Manual, and that black ring binder is the AHMM office manual, detailing all of the working procedures used to undertake its architectural projects, and bringing them together into a single co-ordinated system. An early version of POM was first developed by Victor Kite at YRM as a way of codifying that large practice's way of working, which then became one of the main sources for the RIBA's own Plan of Work. The POM installed by Kite into the AHMM office ranges from Project Inception, Feasibility and Outline Proposals, to Scheme Design, Detail Design and Production Information, through Bills of Quantities, Tender Action and Project Planning, and ends with Operations on Site, Completion and Feedback - over 100 pages standardising office working procedures for every aspect of a project's development, realisation and closure. If a Project Architect in the office wants to know how to approach a problem, POM tells her or him not only what should be done but how to do it.

POM, it has to be said, is not the flashiest of documents. It contains few illustrations beyond diagrams and flow-charts, little text beyond instructions and bullet-points, and no graphic design beyond the use of bold type and underlining. Yet it reveals much about such things as ambition and commitment, that AHMM should seek to produce such a document.

Fig 6 Project Operation Manual

Fig 7 Friday night cash

Fig 8 Advertising for work in the *Ham and High*

Fig 10 One-off internal Christmas
card made by AHMM staff
for the partners, featuring
members of staff – named,
right *(with apologies to
Peter Blake)*

Fig 11 Early publicity

Ultimately, of course, the motive in producing POM is not the system itself but the kind of architecture and architect that springs out of it. POM is part of the office's aim to produce a team of professional architects capable of working together, keeping costs at a minimum and so spending more time actually designing. AHMM architecture and architects would undoubtedly be all the poorer without it.

10

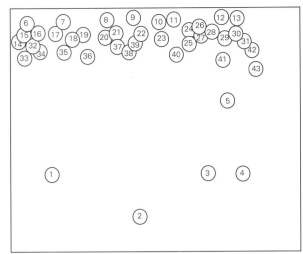

11

FAB FOUR HIT THE RIGHT NOTE

No-one looking at the results of Birmingham's International Design Competition could fail to notice the same four names cropping up among the honours in no fewer than three of the six individual competitions.

Given that the competition attracted 300 entries from 29 countries, this was no small feat.

The quartet (left to right: Peter Morris, Simon Allford, Jonathan Hall and Paul Monaghan) were awarded a £2000 second prize for their scheme for the old Jewellery Quarter, another £2000 second prize (with no first prize awarded) for a leisure development for Holliday Street, and a joint commendation worth £2000 for a project making use of airspace above New Street Station.

And it is not the first time the team has had competition success. The four came together as students to submit a joint scheme for the Diploma at the Bartlett School of Architecture which featured at the RIBA President's Silver Medal show of 1986. They then went around London practices to get a job—as a foursome.

Remarkably they had four or five offers before settling at BDP, where they have been for the last two years—though they also have their own competitions work base in Soho.

'We must have hit the right note with our presentations in the Birmingham competition,' Paul Monaghan said. 'The funny thing is, it was our fourth scheme (for Masshouse Circus), which we were asked to resubmit but which was not placed, that we were happiest with.'

The four lovable mop-tops.

10 AJ 8 March 1989

1. Tony Martin
2. Scott Batty
3. Victor Kite
4. Ben Adams
5. Georgia Tzika
6. Matthew Chisnall
7. Linda McCarney
8. Lawrence Jarvis
9. James Santer
10. Geoffrey Poon
11. Jonathan Crossley
12. Rob Burton
13. Fiona Selmes
14. Christina Fuchs
15. Philip Levack
16. Frank Strathern
17. Will Lee
18. Lee Briscoe
19. Philip Turner
20. Joe Morris
21. Morag Tait
22. Julie Barbier
23. Jayne Chisnall
24. Sarah Hunneyball
25. Charlotte Harrison
26. Yoosung Ok
27. Peter Sargent
28. Jeremy Young
29. Karen Scurlock
30. Maja Koljonen
31. Sonia Grant
32. Felicity Ennis
33. Amy Smith
34. Sam Harvey
35. Steven Morton
36. Ben Gibson
37. Demetra Ryder Runton
38. Tara De Linde
39. Steven Taylor
40. Susi Le Good
41. Ceri Davies
42. Ross Hutchinson
43. Hazel Joseph

5:5.4 Projects X, Y and Z: Sacking the Client

While much of the discussion around professional and social relations in the construction industry centres on notions of promoting partnering, optimising efficiency and maximising mutual benefit, there are undoubtedly times when relationships break down irretrievably. Most extreme (and very rare) is the moment when the architect may have to decide that, whatever the financial and other advantages to pursuing a project, the client is just not worth it. Clients who simply cannot decide a brief, who demand a different building even after completion, who have no aspiration for the project – all of these are potential candidates for dismissal. In such circumstances, sacking the client can be a highly satisfying course of action.

Turnover

Finance costs

Trading profit

Salaries

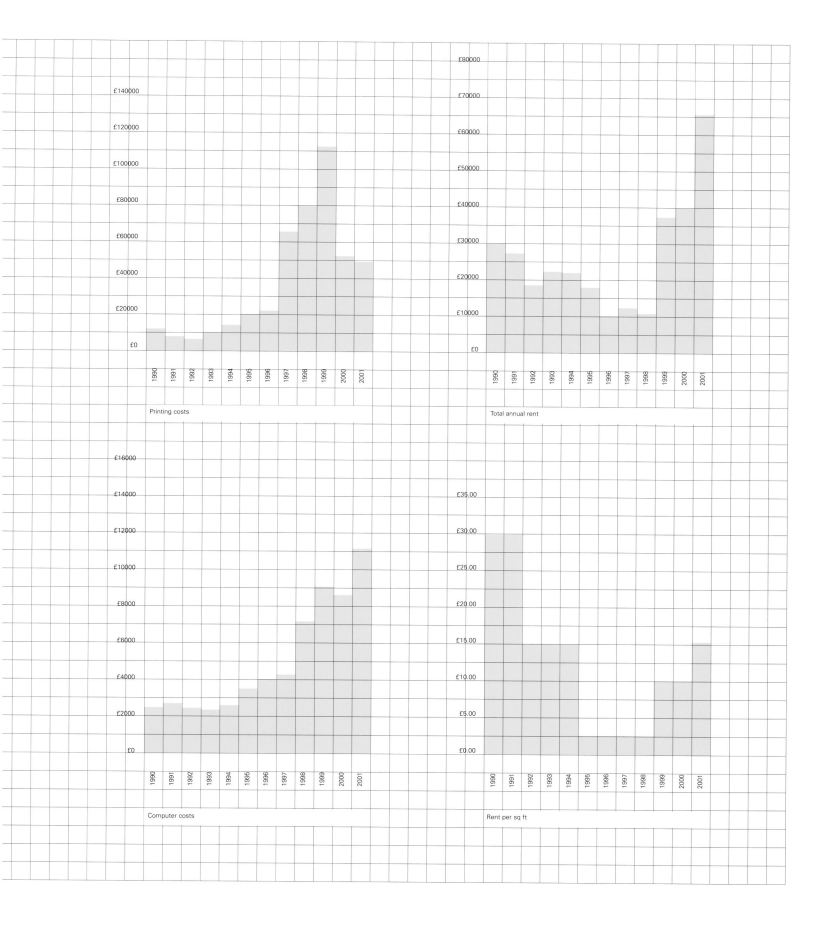

Printing costs

Total annual rent

Computer costs

Rent per sq ft

1989   1990   1991   1992   1993   1994   1995

Ceri Davies

Ceri Davies

Ceri Davies

Cherry Eagleson

Clarissa Richardson

Simon Allford

Jonathan Hall

Leslie Campbell-Wright

Mary Petch

Nicola Hopwood

Paul Monaghan

Peter Crompton

Peter Morris

Rebecca Granger

Sam Harrington-Lowe

Sandra Piesik

Steven Shorter

Susi Le Good

Swiss Bloke

Architecture can be about people

The funny thing is that I am over 20 years older than them, but Simon Allford and Paul Monaghan feel just like old cronies of the '70s or '80s mould – I don't find myself adjusting the conversation to allow for any post-Thatcherist 'cool' or any 'correctness' (political or otherwise).

So the chat is relaxed, open-ended, bitchy, gossipy, conspiratorial, biased, unafraid, mildly sexist, black clothed, London-centric and architectural chat of the best kind: meaning that it's about buildings and stuff. Not about academe (except where one party of a gossip-riff happens to be paid to teach), so they can be gutsily and infinitely critical of every other practice in town… just as I am critical of every other architecture school in England.

Their creative position is an odd one: because it is quintessentially English and terribly, terribly reasonable. 'Liberal' I think I should call it, but their rationale is much tougher than that. Therefore they have brought programmes into the Bartlett that are at right angles to the exploratory/evocative/mystic/dreamy/escapist ground of the other design Units.

Allford and Monaghan love people; they could never exist up a glen or on a mountain top. They're out-and-out 'townies.' Watch them 'work' an evening event, with a smile, a quip and a whisper-in-the-ear for nearly everyone in the room. Iain Borden and I run bets on how many A&M can handle in an evening… 100 ? 150? 200?.

How is it, then, that the stuff coming out the other end is as okay as it is?

What about the mysterious Hall and Morris… not as overt as the lads but personable and bright when they do come out and blink in the sunshine. Maybe they're crouched over the electronic drawing-board or out there in designer wellies? No, not just that. AHMM made a point of sticking to their guns and fronting the four-man team right from the word go! They are as tolerant with each other as they are with their students. It's extraordinary, but these young men-about-business really know all their students, warts and all, gossip and all, hidden talents and all.

So it is that they are living-out my memory of a time (not that long ago) when offices were the product of the personalities and the stories, and when the consequent buildings were able to be the reflection of the likely scenarios running within. Architecture can be about people without being wimpish.

As their office proves.

Peter Cook

| Project 5:6 | > Context and comment |
| Unit 10 | > As AHMM were all Diploma students at the Bartlett, it is fitting that Simon Allford and Paul Monaghan have run first Undergraduate Unit 5 and now Diploma Unit 10 at this architectural school. For over a decade, a highly distinctive contribution has been made to the Bartlett's range of experimental design studios, with Unit 10 now inserting the AHMM agenda into the heart of architectural education. |

Date
1989–Present day

Location
The Bartlett, UCL

Client
The Bartlett, UCL

5:6.1 Programmes

Unit 10 programmes have in successive years dealt with such universal issues as housing, leisure, the architectural profession, work, retail and schooling, while stepping beyond the pure functionalism or form-generation to which such programmes often lead. Unit 10 (U10) work makes sophisticated architectural proposals about how to intervene in the city, work which brings together traditional architectural concerns with form, function, representation and aesthetics with urban issues of the social, economic and developmental aspects of the city.

5:6.2 Conversations

The U10 brand of interaction allows a whole range of possibilities to develop, from AHMM extending and testing their own ideas, to informing and contributing to architectural education with these ideas, to bringing together people from different professions and knowledge bases. A typical U10 crit might thus contain, beside the diploma students and tutors themselves, an architect, a property developer, a journalist, an architectural historian, an engineer and other design tutors. From such combinations new conversations and new ideas about architecture inevitably flow.

1

Fig 1–2 Alasdair Travers

2

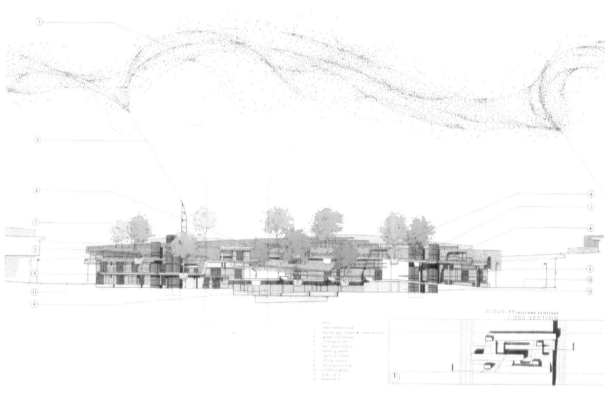

Fig 3–4 Philip Turner

Fig 5–6 Susi le Good

3

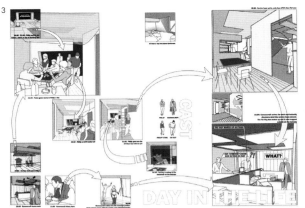

4

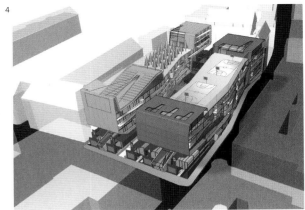

5

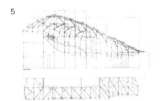

6

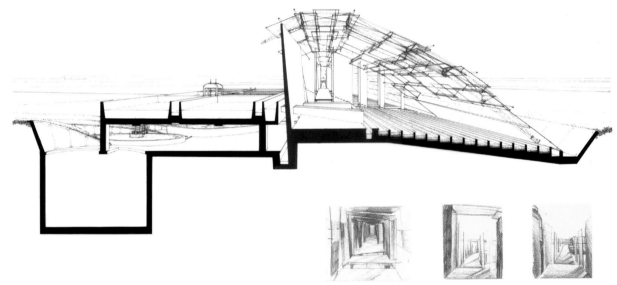

Fig 7–8 Rob Burton

Fig 9 Charlotte Harrison

Fig 10–11 Hazel Joseph

Project 5:7   > Context and comment
Dalston Lane   > Refer to *Surface/Dalston Lane.*

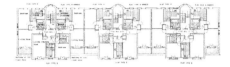

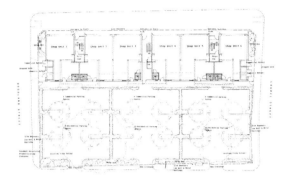

5:7.1 Amending planning

Before AHMM came on to the scene, Peabody had already commissioned a firm of quantity surveyors to design Dalston Lane, and planning permission for a pastiche scheme had duly been gained. This firm was subsequently replaced as designers, however, and AHMM were asked to simply clean up the original design ready for construction. Instead, the office chose to do far more, reinventing the scheme by keeping the shops to the front but pushing the flats to the back, while also changing the section and adding side and rear entrances. Similarly, the whole appearance of the scheme was changed to an architecture that contributed much more to Hackney than had the tired gestures of the original proposal.

The real invention, however, was not so much architectural as to do with the planning system. Despite reworking the overall appearance of the apartment block, and making some large alterations to the internal spatial arrangement, the office were able to get their scheme through planning not as a new proposal but as a simple planning amendment, thus saving large sums of time and money.

Further benefits from a close interaction with the planning system emerged when the Head of Urban Design in the local borough supported the office's suggestion of using a chequer-board pattern to break up the mass of building. The result was the distinctive blue and white grid which now provides such a purposeful presence on the Hackney streetscape.

3

Fig 1 Original plans produced by
      another design company

Fig 2 Dalston Lane view

Fig 3 A local resident with
      more than a passing knowledge
      of architecture

Fig 4 Side view

Fig 5 Opposition to scheme
      in the local press

4

5:7.2 Turnaround

Not everyone was happy about this decision.
Although there had been consultation with local
residents about the scheme in its earlier stages,
AHMM did not need to return to this forum to
discuss the chequerboard grid.

As a result, when the scaffolding around the building
came down, one local councillor nearly drove off the
road when he saw it, and immediately insisted it be
repainted or even pulled down. This councillor, along
with other residents, soon appeared in a local paper,
protesting against what they called a 'hideous' piece
of architecture.

In order to diffuse the situation, Peabody and AHMM
arranged to meet local residents in a nearby hall. At
this meeting, many of those present started off by
complaining in the strongest possible of terms,
demanding that changes be made. The office went to
some lengths to explain that although local residents
had a right to be consulted, they did not in fact have
a right to dictate what all architecture should look like.
An ugly impasse seemed certain.

Then a rare moment in consultation occurred.
Firstly, a local resident stated how much she liked
the Dalston Lane block for giving lively interest and
focal point to what was otherwise a drab and
depressingly uniform street. And then another local
resident, with seemingly more than a passing knowledge
of architecture, pointed out that much architecture is
different to its surroundings, including, for example,
the very building in which they were meeting (an arts
and crafts-style, red brick mansion block, sited
completely off grid, and entirely at odds with most of
the local architecture). He argued for lots of new
buildings, and that what the borough of Hackney really
deserved was not dull mediocrity but unique and high
quality architecture – like Dalston Lane. The effect
was immediate, and the meeting ended with a vote in
support of the new building – a complete turnaround
of opinion in the course of two hours.

5

Project 5:8	> Context and comment
Walsall Bus Station	> Bus station with satellite bus-stand and adjacent public square.

Date
1995–2000

> Central to the looming presence of Walsall Bus Station is an enormous elliptical roof, precisely designed through a careful collaboration between AHMM and structural engineer Neil Thomas of Atelier One.

Location
Walsall

> Through this collaboration, the original steel roof construction envisaged at competition stage changed to a concrete canopy punctured by numerous twisted roof-top cones. The two main advantages of the concrete roof solution – a simpler self-finish and a greater flexibility in the positioning of the supporting tree-like pillars – had to be reconciled against extremely complex engineering calculations and construction techniques.

Client
Centro

> The following text is written by Atelier One, and first appeared in an Architects' Journal feature on the Walsall Bus Station.

1

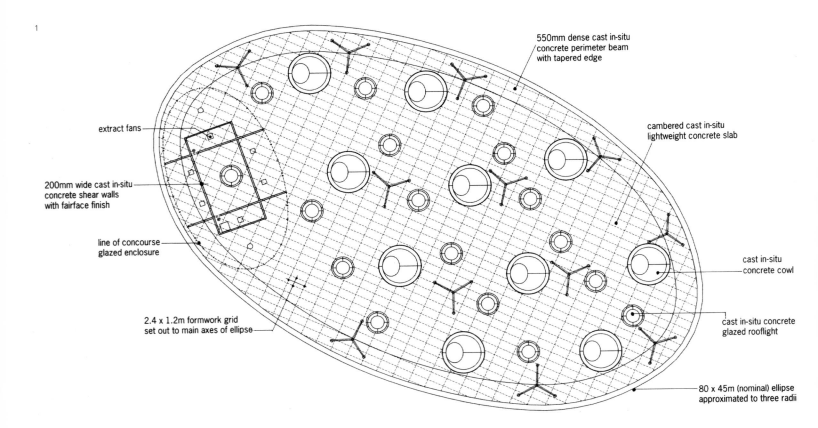

extract fans

200mm wide cast in-situ concrete shear walls with fairface finish

line of concourse glazed enclosure

2.4 x 1.2m formwork grid set out to main axes of ellipse

550mm dense cast in-situ concrete perimeter beam with tapered edge

cambered cast in-situ lightweight concrete slab

cast in-situ concrete cowl

cast in-situ concrete glazed rooflight

80 x 45m (nominal) ellipse approximated to three radii

Fig 1 Reflected plan
of canopy soffit

Fig 2 Stress contour plot
of canopy, giving
the distribution
across the surface.

5:8.1 Finite element analysis

The structural challenge is to reconcile an 80 x 40m elliptical canopy at a height of eight metres, supported on columns positioned between bus lanes, giving a significant variation in spans across the surface. Because it is impossible to impose a rational grid on the structure that will distribute loads evenly back to column positions, we decided to consider the roof as a plate as opposed to a series of beams, where we can compensate the stiffness of the plate based on the forces within particular regions. Concrete was chosen to allow this principle to be developed in detail, whereby additional reinforcement is added locally within the slab and edge beam, but the depth of the concrete is uniform across the slab and around the perimeter edge beam.

The spans between columns vary and, in effect, the slab spans in all directions with an uneven distribution of forces – so deflections are critical. We developed a finite element analysis model assuming a flat slab to understand the overall behaviour of the roof. It was realised that to limit deflections a much stiffer structure was required than a simple flat slab, so a three metre-wide edge beam is added, which runs continuously around the perimeter of the canopy.

The 325mm-deep roof slab is punctured by a series of five metre diameter cowls and smaller roof lights.

The roof lights are not structural, but the conical cowls play a significant role in giving additional stiffness to the flat slab. Because of their shape it was decided to use entire depth of the cowls (rather like an upstand beam) as an enhancement to the stiffness of the flat slab.

The slab area is specified as lightweight concrete simply to reduce the dead weight of the structure, and the edge beam is specified as C50 normal weight concrete. The other critical issue was the method of depropping the canopy. The principle was to lower the entire surface evenly, thereby avoiding throwing additional loads into depropped spans adjacent to propped spans, which would not achieve the balance and continuity over the column positions.

The lateral stability of the canopy is achieved solely by the concrete walls within the concourse building, which connect directly into the slab and resist any rotation of the canopy. The steel trees are then designed to prop the canopy vertically. The steel trees support significant areas of roof with spans up to 23 metres. The branches are formed from flat plates to form triangular sections that taper in both plan and elevation. The difficult connection to the slab and load transfer is achieved by using a series of hollowed spigots through which to run plates and plates bearing on to the concrete with additional areas of shear reinforcement.

2 Displacement Contours of DZ

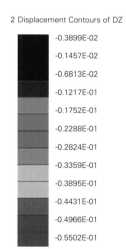

■	-0.3899E-02
■	-0.1457E-02
■	-0.6813E-02
■	-0.1217E-01
■	-0.1752E-01
■	-0.2288E-01
■	-0.2824E-01
■	-0.3359E-01
■	-0.3895E-01
■	-0.4431E-01
■	-0.4966E-01
■	-0.5502E-01

6:0 Spacing

Perhaps more than any other part of architecture, the role of space and the architect's engagement with it lies at the heart of architectural design procedures. Space is what architects create, configure and dream about, turning architecture from being a purely two-dimensional and visual affair into a matter of three-dimensions, lively events, and imaginative modelling. But if space is one of the fundamental concerns of architecture, what exactly is it?

Space is no easy thing to grasp. It is partly physical, being the actual built space of rooms, building and cities that we see all around us. It is partly an activity, being all the various actions undertaken and all the energies disposed as we go about our lives. It is partly representational, being all the various codes – from texts and classifications, to diagrams and drawings, to mappings and equations – that we deploy in order to intellectually codify and display space. And it is partly experiential, being all of the phenomenological and perceptual ways in which we experience architecture and the city. Space, then, is far more than the drawing of lines on paper; for good architecture to occur space must be comprehended in the full range of its possible existences, and brought together by the architect – to the best of her or his abilities – into coherent possibilities and opportunities.

The problem for the architect – if not for architecture as a whole – is that he or she does not necessarily have (indeed, rarely has) complete control over the production of space. Other professionals, other urban dwellers, other individuals also have a say in the complex process of making space. Yet this does not mean that the architect can do nothing. Indeed, the opposite may be true, the very complexity of space offering the architect the chance to undertake actions and operations which can help to release the possibility of space in architecture.

These possibilities – and hence the architectural techniques necessary to encourage them – are neither singular nor static. A whole tool kit of spacing operations is required, each with its own modus operandi, and each with a distinct spatial effect and possibility.

The following examples are but some of these tools, and but a few of these spatial possibilities: space which is tidied, clarified and interlinked; space oriented to both inward light and internal contents; space which is deliberately uncomfortable and unattractive; space which is precisely tessellated and intensively compacted; space as conceptual framework, facilitating overall design development; space as sectional explosion; space as closure and introversion; space which is over-sized; space as filter or mechanism for the exchange of view; space as companion to surface texture; and space as event and activity. None of these are finite or closed tactics; each has its own effects, both predictable and accidental. All are space as architecture.

Project 6:1	**> Context and comment**
Clearwater Yard	> A small office, positioned just off the extremely busy Camden High Street.
Date	> The site, a former timber yard, was excavated by nearly 2 metres in order to provide a total
2000–02	floor area of 1,275 m².
Location	> The project demands a reconciliation of several seemingly contradictory oppositions: private and
Camden, London	public, bustle and rest, dynamism and calmness, security and openness, anonymity and publicity.
Client	
Latitude Investments	
Limited	

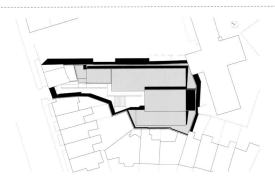

Site plan   1:1250

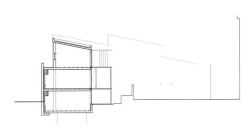

Section through upper courtyard

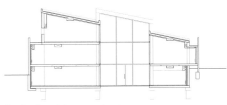

Section through lower courtyard

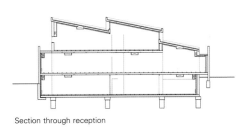

Section through reception

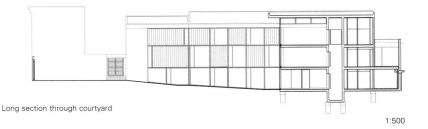

Ground floor plan

Long section through courtyard

1:500

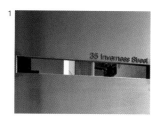

Fig 1 Entrance screen
opening allowing
glimpses of the
building beyond

Fig 2 Opaque and
transparent glazing

Fig 3 Entrance courtyard
viewed from building

Fig 4 Upper office floor

6:1.1 Closure

The scheme adopted first makes one major move: the closure of the site by a screen wall across its street end. The office is immediately protected behind this element, affording all the buffering it requires from the constant madness of the fashionable world of Camden outside. The immediate face is of restraint and absence, with only a hint of the bold confidence and presence which lies beyond.

6:1.2 Aperture

Despite this apparent closure, aperture also occurs. Firstly, an opening in the screen wall provides visual entry into the space beyond. Like a discovery by Alice in *Through the Looking-Glass*, the office becomes a hidden delight, awaiting discovery by the more inquisitive of urban flâneurs. Secondly, physical entry into the space leads not directly to a building, but into an extended courtyard-come-garden. What at first appears to be a pure boundary (the screen wall) thus immediately yields to an intermediary space of openness before the office entrance proper is discovered at the very rear of the site. This is a place of real charm, with varied landscape levels working against the sudden colour of the building, with spatiality working against objects, of complex inner character contained behind a subtle outer screen.

6:1.3 Vectors of law

The building placed here is far from accidental. Surrounded on all sides by proximate and demanding neighbours, Clearwater Yard uses these conditions not as constraints but as stimulants with which to generate its overall massing and internal spatiality. To the west and north-west, the close proximity of late Georgian housing led to several impositions regarding height and views out – hence the sloping roofs lifting up and away towards the east of the site, and hence the language of alternating opaque and transparent glass, punctuated by splashes of colour, on the façades. The domestic neighbours are also now rewarded by new views onto the sloping sedum roof. To the east, a neighbouring school meant that no windows could be placed right on the boundary line of the site – hence the negotiation to step back the building line by a metre at the highest level, thus allowing a strip window to be inserted down the length of the office. To the south, the same school is joined by more housing (include the private residence of one of the borough planners) – hence the inclusion of highly expensive noise attenuators, reducing the sound of the heating and cooling plant to almost nothing.

Fig 5 Unisex toilets

Fig 6 Stairwell with 'supergraphics' by Studio Myerscough

Fig 7 View across courtyard to sedum roofscape

Opposite: Entrance screen hints at the prescence of the new building beyond

Page 178 Night-time transparency

Page 179 Façade detailing

6:1.4 Vectors of sight

Within the overall massing of the project, a complicated internal game of views and sightlines emerges. This comes from three conditions. Firstly, the U-shaped courtyard arrangement creates a series of views from the interior out into the courtyard, and then back in again to the internal spaces of building on the other side of the interstitial gap. Secondly, the alternating and variable nature of the cladding means that such views are never predictable, certain or fixed. Thirdly, the decision to make what is effectively the basement level into the ground floor/reception floor renders greater verticality into the scheme, so that views across the courtyard are often as much down or up as they are across or between. The result is an intricate space, one in which the relatively free-flowing nature of the floorspace is both enhanced and partially contradicted by its less direct visual counterpart – real space and visual space are not exactly the same here, but contrapuntal partners within a sophisticated, choreographed dance.

6:1.5 Inner world/other world

Once properly encountered, the beguiling architecture Clearwater Yard creates the sense of being at once within an inner private world and simultaneously transported somewhere else entirely. The materials palette of Reglit opaque glass, green and yellow panels, pre-cast concrete and precise formwork patterns creates an atmosphere of interiority, seclusion and solitude, calmly withdrawn from Camden and its impossibly in-your-face hyper-hip-frenzy. And yet other aspects of the scheme are dynamically transformative, for the cascading roof planes, chequerboard patterning, floor-identifying supergraphics, light-flooded volumes and some surprising social innovations such as single sex toilets with piped music and digital fish tanks all combine to create an almost Californian ambience. Calmer details, such as the Miesian simplicity of the bespoke cladding frames and the gentle colouration of the exposed concrete ceilings and columns, further add to the sense of theatre. This is a world of sun, trees and modernism.

Taken as a complete experience, Clearwater Yard acts as perpetual space-transformer, flipping the visitor firstly from the conditions of a busy street to that of a calm garden, then from that nature-filled courtyard to an interior bright modernism, and then once again from that hard English architecture to a more relaxed West Coast spatiality. It is not an easy place to leave.

Project 6:2
Mallett-Catcheside
House

Date
1994–96

Location
Canonbury, London

Client
Lee Mallett and
Kim Catcheside

> **Context and comment**
> Private house.

> A run-down four-storey Georgian property in the up-market Canonbury area of London bought by Lee Mallett (then editor of *Building Design* magazine) and media broadcaster Kim Catcheside, for themselves and their two children. Converting the property meant not only stripping out the ground floor shop but making it spatially and socially more suitable for a modern family.

> Mallett's interest in property development dictated that revenue-generation was also an ultimate aim – a condition more than met when the 1996 purchase-plus-conversion costs were substantially improved upon when the property was sold a few years later

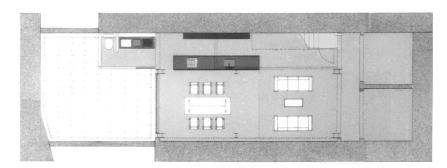

Lower ground floor plan

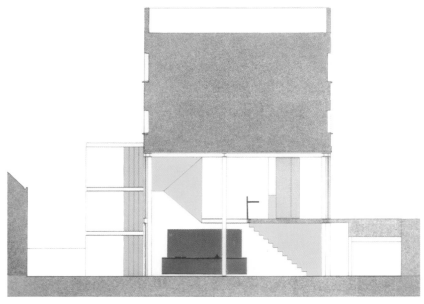

Section   1:200

6:2.1 Section

The traditional Georgian house conversion typically involves 'knocking through' a couple of adjoining rooms, a new kitchen and bathroom, and perhaps even the addition of a basement extension or attic conversion. The spatial tactics undertaken at the Mallett-Catcheside house were, by contrast, more dramatic in nature. The whole ground floor was cut out, and with the advice of Nick Hanika of Price & Myers a two-storey high steel structure – effectively a gigantic but cost effective table top with four legs – was inserted into the basement, while a huge double-height window floods it with light. A three storey rear tower was added to hold utilities, a study and bathroom. Upper rooms were left largely untouched.

The result is a complete sectional reconfiguration of the conventional terraced house: an unrestricted double height lower zone, offering open space and social interaction; a more normal set of bedrooms up above, offering containment and privacy; plus a services stack offering internalisation and isolation.

6:2.2 Event

The lower basement space is the dominant space of the newly reworked house, offering loft-like living but without the impracticality of completely open-plan living. Apart from the privacy of the cellular bedrooms up above, the lower space is also extended out into the sub-pavement vaults to create cavernous storage area for toys and other child-related paraphernalia, while the tiny rear yard is similarly incorporated into the house via the full-width, two-storey window wall.

The fit-out uses inexpensive plywood flooring, painted standard steel elements and an off-the-peg kitchen to create an inexpensive yet expansive atmosphere. Rather than a gallery-like display of objects, this is an arrangement meant for events-in-space: rambling dinners, kids riding around on trikes, parties, breakfasts, people slumped on chairs and sofas, and chatting. In this house, the openness of the space leads to a similar openness of movements and actions.

6:2.3 Texture

Spatial reconfiguration often leads to unexpected pleasures. When the concrete infill on one of the party walls was hammered off, it disclosed a zone of rough masonry. Quickly dubbed by the 'whispering wall' for its poetic everyday qualities, this newly revealed texture was left to stand untreated, both as an autonomous surface of textured beauty, and as a device for the deliberate delimitation of space.

6:2.4 Television

After some argument with the local planners (who misguidedly asked for a Georgian style domestic ground floor window to be 'reinstated' where in fact no such element had ever existed at this particular property), it was agreed that a modern landscape-format rectangular window could be used on the street front.

For passers-by, this element provides a view from the ground level down into the unexpectedly large basement space. Conversely, for the house's residents the self-same element creates a television-screen like vista, with a changing cast of characters appearing, disappearing and re-appearing at different times of the day and week. As Mallett described it, this is "our very own soap opera. People keep coming back to see what's occurring now... Sometimes they smile and wave and sometimes they disappear rapidly for fear of intruding. It gets a bit much at half term when we've got seven kids using us as entertainment for half-hour stretches. So we got an electric blind."

On pragmatism

If I was permitted only one word to describe AHMM's work then it would have to be a seemingly dull one – 'pragmatism.' This is at the root of all the practice has achieved, and, contrary to what pragmatism might imply, it has proved to be a sustained creative wellspring for them.

The only AHMM work I can really speak authoritatively about is the conversion of a property in Canonbury which my wife Kim and I commissioned from them in the mid-1990s when I was editing Building Design (I can feel architects everywhere flinching as they recall those horrendous domestic commissions). It was a breathtaking bit of architectural thinking that persuaded us to let them rip out the dry-rot ridden ground floor and all the basement partitioning of this former shop, demolish half the rear elevation and derelict addition, dig out the front elevation at basement level (so the under-pavement brick arches could be incorporated in the yawning cavity thus created) and to stick in a giant new steel frame with glass walls.

Living on overgrown Acro Props for a year while expecting a second child is character-forming. But the result more than compensated us for the anguish. At a stroke we re-foundationed the house and created a fab loft-style space in a Victorian terraced house, with a dramatic little office perched in the upper levels of the new living space and an entrance hall also hanging in it, while having four bedrooms over the lot. And, what's more, it was much, much cheaper than repairing what was already there – we know, because we did the figures. That's what I mean by pragmatism. We got a great piece of dramatic architecture for less that the cost of a boring refurb. A problem solved by the creation of something new. That's when architecture really works.

My usual whinge about why we sold the place is that (as many couples find) bureaulandschaft living gets difficult when the kids get bicycles and even noisier toys. I should also mention that 800 people came to see it on 'Open House' day, and I suspect that AHMM's scheme helped more than double the value of the property.

The other building I want to comment on is Great Notley school. AHMM's work had always appeared to me fundamentally orthogonal - square (this was pre-Walsall Bus Station). Yet their pragmatism here led AHMM to a kind of rationalised deconstructivism and a radical triangular plan that for me synthesised everything that was going on in contemporary architecture and produced a really great little school. My favourite British building of the 1980s was Tony Fretton's Lisson Gallery. I would argue that Great Notley was the best building of the 1990s by any British architect. I think AHMM have bags more to show us and ambition to match. Also their academic involvement, principally with the Bartlett, seems to be sustaining the vitality of their architecture (and helping to put experience back into students) in a way that larger more successful practices should take note of. This too is a pragmatic process.

Lee Mallett

Project 6:3	> **Context and comment**
Barbican	> Reconfiguration of the public spaces of an arts centre.

Date
2000 onwards

Location
Barbican, London

Client
Barbican Centre

> First designed by the architects Chamberlin Powell and Bon from the the 1950s to the 1980s, the brutalist concrete structures of the Barbican Estate in London offer a remarkable concentration of residential, art, education and leisure facilities in the centre of the capital. Foremost among them is the Barbican Centre, a multi-arts and conference venue, much loved by London arts-goers.

> Despite a number of attempts at improvement, the Barbican Centre's internal spaces have long suffered from an impossible confusion of entangled and contradictory entrances, routes and signage – producing a constant flow of withering criticism and complaint.

Site plan   1:2500

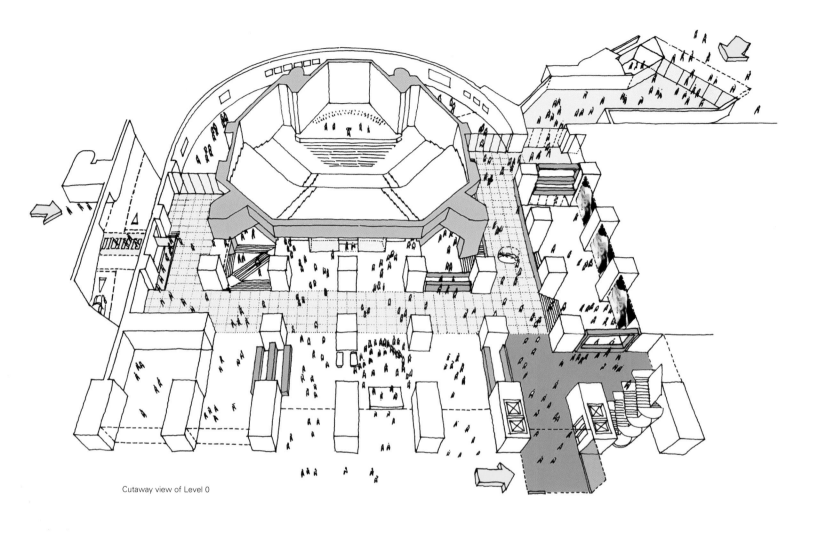

Cutaway view of Level 0

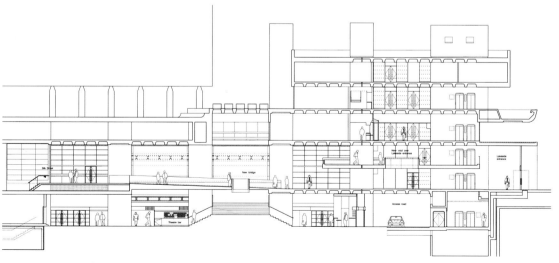

Long section through bridge

1:500

Fig 1 Existing foyer space

Fig 2 'Baffling Barbican to
       get £6m facelift'

Fig 3 Silk Street entrance

6:3.1 Unification

The internal spaces of the Barbican are simply, as the BBC has described it, baffling. The numerous entrances, frequent changes of level, partially connecting lifts and stairways, truncated corridors, obstructed sightlines and uncertain signs of the original Chamberlin Powell and Bon scheme conflate with a redesign by Pentagram in the early 1990s to produce a set of spaces that constantly conspire to infuriate even the most frequent of visitors.

On the other hand, these self-same spaces have the potential to offer a myriad of social opportunities: not just for concerts and art galleries, but also for eating, drinking, strolling through, and chance encounters. These are the demands which visitors would like to make of the Barbican, but which at present cannot be met.

The response has therefore been to render the main spaces of the Centre more intuitively comprehensible to visitors, while simultaneously preserving its dominant architectural characteristics: the existing Pentagram-designed raised bridge obscuring the side theatre auditorium is removed, and replaced with a more appropriate structure; the Silk Street and Lakeside entrances are clarified and the north-south route through is emphasised; the Lakeside Terrace is reworked into a more intensive zone of leisure activity; new foyer arrangements are inserted for proper dining and drinking, as well as to allow private functions to occasionally take over a whole interior section; new signage, information points and route co-ordination further enhance this process of unification, reducing the scheme's inherently dislocating tendencies; and the lower public spaces are stripped back to their original state, restoring much of building's modernist integrity.

The result is an unlocking of socio-spatial potential. Reconfiguration of space leads to a simultaneous integration and diversification of human activities. Coherence engenders differential existence.

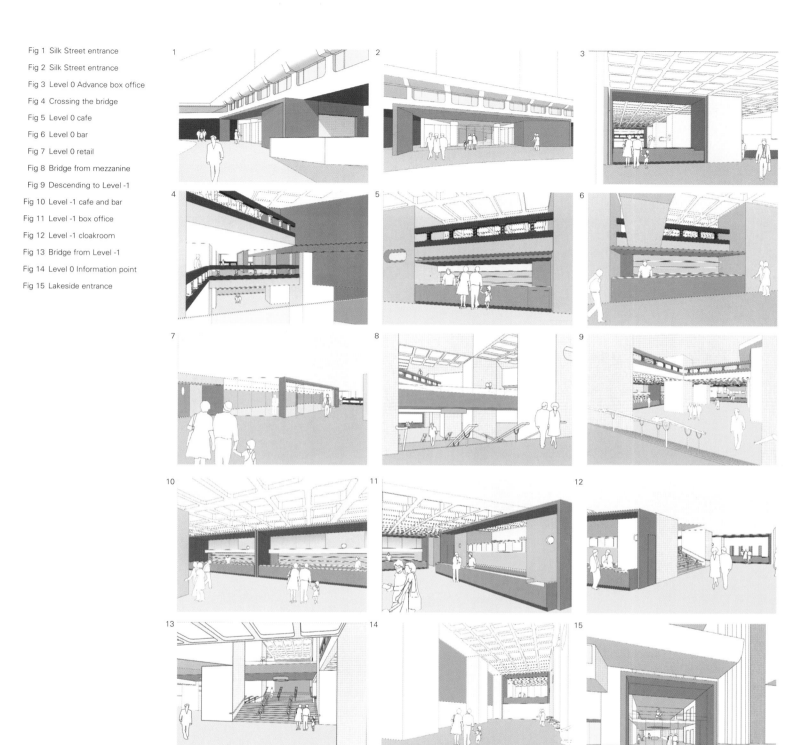

Project 6:4
Private Apartment

Date
1995–1996

Location
North London

Client
Beryl and David Allford

> **Context and comment**
> A £165,000 fit out of a large apartment in a former warehouse from the 1930s.

> Loft-style living at its most luxurious: 200m² for a couple, with a 16-18 metre deep plan, and south-facing views onto one of London's most beautiful squares.

> The territories given over to living, kitchen/dining, master bedroom, guest bedroom and the study/library are almost entirely fluid, completely devoid of circulation with separation, when required, being provided by over-size pivoted and sliding doors.

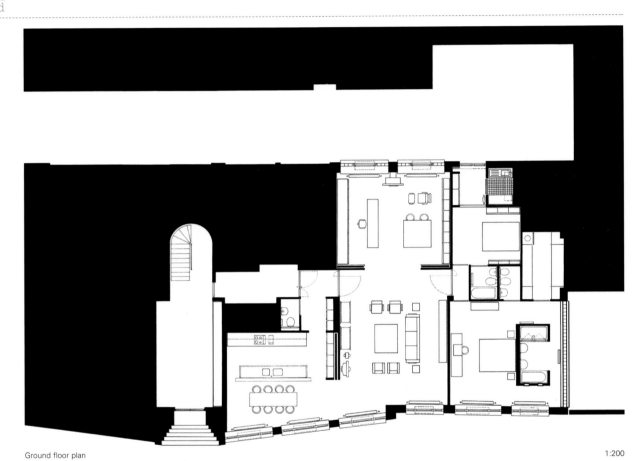

Ground floor plan

1:200

6:4.1 Stage Set

The apartment boasts a highly rational yet open plan, and although this architecture appears to be without artifice, a number of carefully wrought tactics and devices have been deployed to give this effect. For example, the minimal use of east-west walls combined with variable ceiling heights and both clear- and opaque-glass windows allows for the maximum penetration of light. Throughout the apartment, specialist shop-fitters fabricated exact shadow-gaps, while the massive sliding doors providing demarcation between the living and study areas are equipped with bespoke handles which allow a grip to be obtained even when pushed back into their *poché niches*.

The overall result is a series of flexible stage sets, precisely configured to create an extremely generous space for an elegantly social yet easy-going couple.

Fig 3 Kitchen and
      dining area

Fig 4 View from study
      to living area

Opposite Sliding doors
with bespoke handles

3

6:4.2 Discomfort
Everyone needs occasional privacy and isolation, and
the apartment owners were worried that its central
London location would prove just too tempting to
visiting family and friends. For this reason there is only
one guest bedroom, which is also made singularly
small and unattractive, and is placed in the least
desirable corner of the plot. Through this gesture, the
owners' desire for solitude can be all but guaranteed.

6:4.3 Display
While overnight visitors are positively discouraged at
the apartment, another kind of more long term 'guest'
is very much catered for: the numerous pieces of art
and furniture which the owners have accumulated
over the course of their life together.

The apartment is thus precisely designed to
accommodate a number of these elements,
including, for example: an office table and chairs,
and a Chinese black lacquer cabinet that previously
sat in one of the owners' office; a cabinet from an
earlier London flat; two Breuer chairs placed next
to the television; a Max Bill designed sofa, plus four
accompanying Danish seats; a Richard Hamilton
picture and a series of Paolozzi prints, the latter's
colour being somewhat jokily picked up in the green
Formica of the nearby kitchen; and a Joe Tilson piece
located in the living area but carefully positioned to
be viewed from the dining area.

The apartment is thus in part constituted as a series
of *mises-en-scène* for these elements. Life and colour
are here provided by art, furniture and event, set
against the more neutral spatial theatre of the
architecture itself.

4

Project 6:5
Great Notley
Primary School

> **Context and comment**
> Refer to *Landing/Great Notley Primary School.*

Fig 1 The only corridor
in the school

Fig 2 Trademark view
of the triangular
building's 'prow'

Fig 3 Study models developing
building form

6:5.1 Intensity

The intensity of the plan arrangement is considerable, packing into a single shape an extraordinary range of rooms and other spaces. For example, think of a school and most people think of corridors – long stretches of linear circulation space, necessary for the repetitive transfer of hordes of children but highly wasteful in terms of floor space and, of course, energy consumption. Great Notley, by contrast, has virtually no corridor space at all apart from one passage running across the backs of the classrooms. Similarly, the roofed central hall – rather than an open atrium – enables another more useful space to be incorporated, simultaneously providing for assembly, transfer and air movement.

As a result of these kinds of spatial intensity and refinement, the school's spaces are almost entirely free of corridors, offering a kind of immediacy to the way people relate to each other within the building and, simultaneously, savings in money and energy.

6:5.2 Schema

Although the triangular plan offers, on the one hand, a way of refining the spaces of the Great Notley Primary School into a new perfect and crystal-like arrangement, on the other hand it also offers something very different. By adopting the triangle as a much broader, conceptual schema, the project as a whole is imparted with an overall, loose-fit framework. In short, the triangle figure allows architectural experimentation while simultaneously instilling a kind of open constraint and control into the design development process.

Site plan   1:10,000

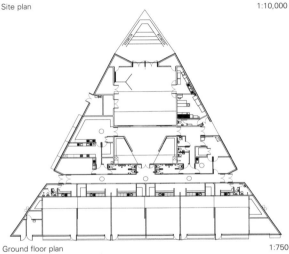

Ground floor plan   1:750

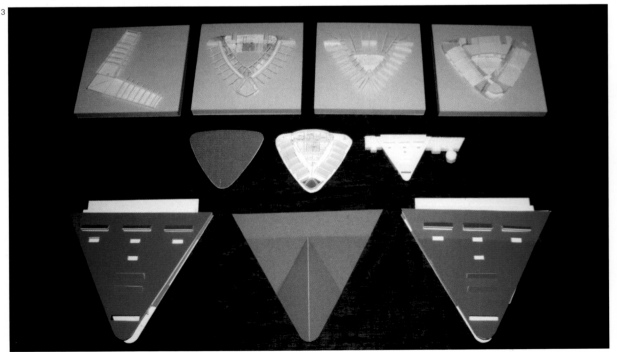

Fig 4 View to main hall
from central space

Fig 5 Main hall

Fig 6 View to central space
from main hall

Project 6:6
Raines Dairy

Date
1998–2003

Location
Stoke Newington,
London

Client
Peabody Trust

> **Context and comment**
> Affordable housing and live-work units.

> An experimental venture for the Peabody Trust, providing shared ownership homes. At the base sits 400m² of live-work space, above which are located 53 single-storey apartments.

> The whole scheme is built from modular principles developed by the office and Peabody into an attenuated version of prefabricated and standardised architecture.

> Raines Dairy partly connects to Peabody's temporary housing project also being worked on by the office. Refer to Interacting/MoMo Apartments.

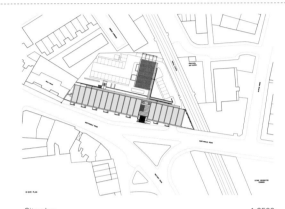

Site plan   1:2500

South elevation

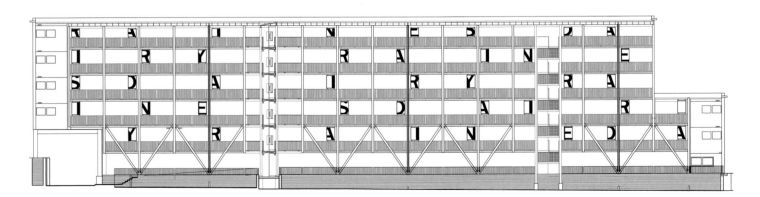

North elevation   1:400

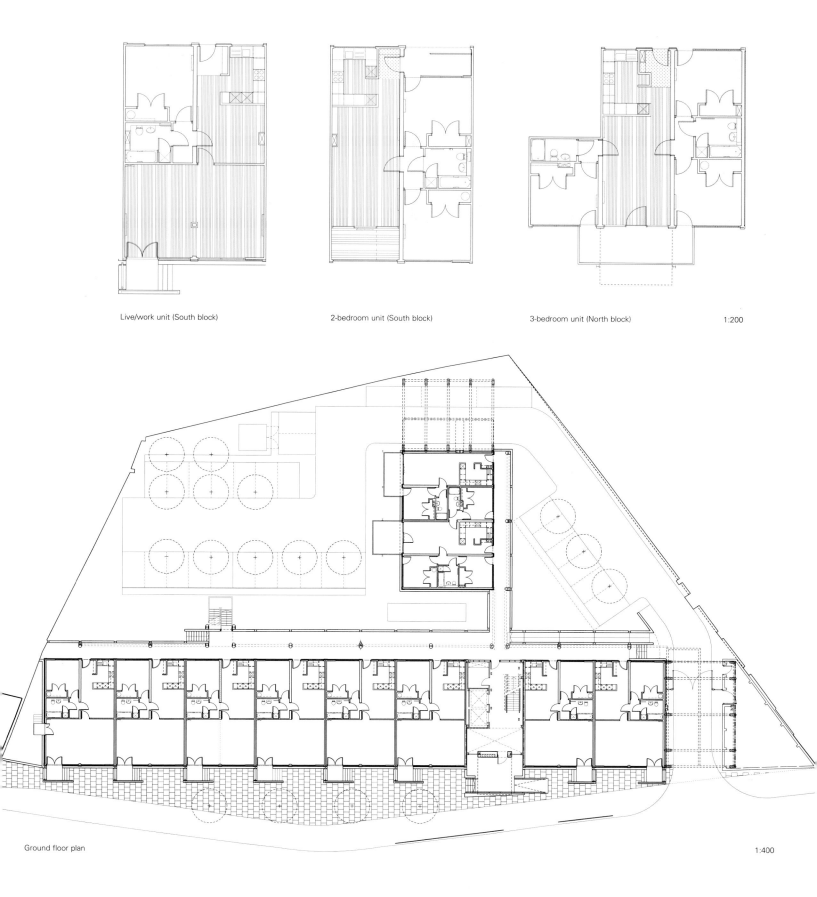

Live/work unit (South block)

2-bedroom unit (South block)

3-bedroom unit (North block)

1:200

Ground floor plan

1:400

Fig 1 Pre-fabricated module
in factory

Fig 2 Computer view from
Northwold Road

6:6.1 Modularisation

Some earlier modular housing has three modules per
dwelling, requiring cutting across, cladding and other
work to be carried out on site. At Raines Dairy, just
two modules are combined with the largest possible
space (4.2m wide x 18m long) that can be transported
on a conventional truck without expensive escort.

The ambition at Raines Dairy is to include as much
architecture as possible into individual modules. Eventually,
modules should include all cladding, balconies, sun
screens etc. such that, beyond foundations and
landscaping, all that will remain to be done on site
will be to fit covering strips between modules.

The result is a modular system of architectural
production that can be almost entirely factory built,
transported straight to site whenever required, and
simply craned into place.

6:6.2 Site benefits

The benefits of such methods of production are not
only confined to the object itself; site conditions can
also be considerably improved. By pre-fabricating the
architecture, much of the scaffolding, wooden
walkways and other temporary aspects of a typical
construction site are kept to a minimum, thus allowing
work to proceed faster, more cheaply and more safely.
Indeed, other aspects of the particular Raines Dairy

site more or less demanded such an approach to construction. The adjacent railway line meant that it would have been extremely difficult to build using normal methods, for fear of a piece of construction equipment, material or tool being dropped on to the tracks and de-railing a speeding train.

6:6.3 Patterning

Despite the use of only two modules, the schema adopted allows for an unusual degree of adaptability and flexibility, across three-bedroom, two-bedroom, one-bedroom and live-work units. Devices such as using bedrooms as fire escape routes and module-crossing through clipping in a double-skinned door set allows the modules to be handed, while the slipped plan provides for both a small front garden and rear balcony. In addition, the office has worked with colourist Charlotte Ingle to give each of the 62 balconies a subtly different colour.

Apart from extremely high densities, which at 196 dwellings (620 habitable rooms) per hectare are over twice that normally allowed by the local borough's Unitary Development Plan, particular aesthetic benefits are also generated by this arrangement. Unlike the completely homogenous strips of windows,

doors and balconies often created by conventional standardised housing, the fact that each module contains its own service duct means that Raines Dairy can accommodate considerable variation in elevational pattern, thus recalling the tradition of Tecton and Berthold Lubetkin within English social housing.

6:6.4 Urban presence

Raines Dairy sits in a fairly grim urban location. Bounded by a railway line to the east and a busy one-way road system to the south, its immediate context is the typical detritus of a north London borough: litter, graffiti, fly-posters, unkempt grass and weeds, municipal notices and battered railings. What the new apartment block adds into this unpromising scenario is a radical, bold insertion, a vital disjunction to the grey and brick surroundings of Hackney, with hugely-present metal and colour facades pinned to the ground by live-work units spreading employment and activity into the neighbourhood. Whether Raines Dairy indeed succeeds in provoking a micro-regeneration of this neighbourhood only the next decade or so will tell; but for the moment it offers a real chance for many residents to dwell and toil in the area, and is not afraid to say so architecturally.

3
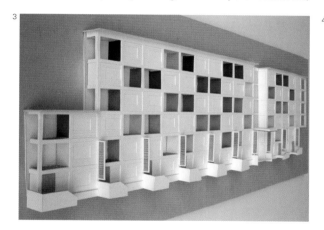

4

A factor of change distinguishes their buildings

Over and above their mastery of seemingly simple 3-D forms, A+H+2M appear to have a continuous delight in the economy of materials they use, allied to the speed of building processes they select. Introducing speed into the very process of building achieves economy of architecture in a form intelligible to all who use their buildings. A factor of change distinguishes their buildings.

Two very disparate buildings exemplify this quality. One is the CASPAR housing in Birmingham, where there is an awareness of time of day. The glazed central area generates a variety of shadows, cast by the access platforms.

In Great Notley Primary School in Essex the change is related to the age and size of the pupils, and to the variety of recognisable access, both internally and externally. In relation to the staff, a range of change is afforded by the available alteration of use of various teaching services. In both types of building, qualities of familiarity through usage contrast with degrees of recognition for both groups of users.

The environmental range of social changes is anticipated and recognised in both buildings. In the Housing, recognition is allied to familiarity and security; whereas in the School such social change achieves for pupils a degree of excitement different from the home environment, while for the staff such change enables a familiarity of teaching methods to be honed, according to the particular staff and curricula deemed beneficial at any one time.

Cedric Price

Project 6:7
Otemon Housing

> Context and comment
> Competition entry for an apartment block.

Date
1990

> Invited competition organised by a Japanese development corporation looking to identify young architectural talent in the UK.

Location
Fukuoka, Japan

> The AHMM entry, coming at the tail end of architecture's love-hate affair with postmodernism, is determinedly modernist in character, using a Corbusian void and hanging garden arrangement around which to compose four flats per floor.

Client
TED Associates

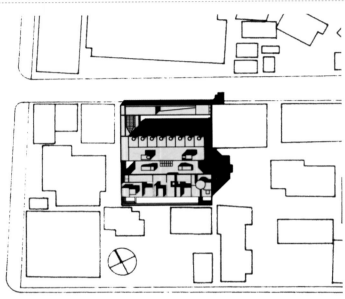

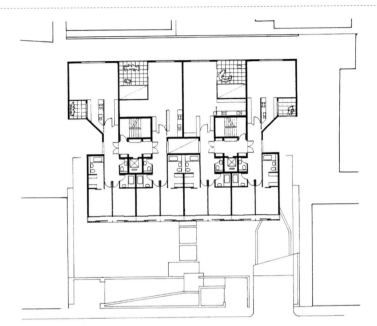

Site plan   1:1250

Typical floor plan

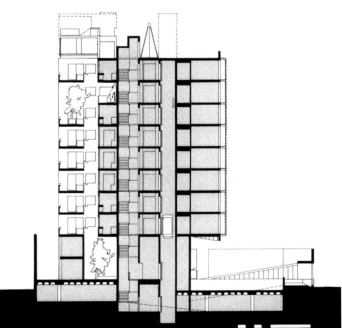

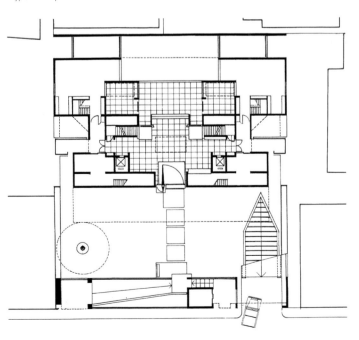

Section

Ground floor plan   1:500

Fig 1 Samurai helmet

Fig 2 Silhouette

Fig 3 Screens

Fig 4 Street view

6:7.1 Filter

Far removed from Le Corbusier's Immeubles Villas concept is, however, a very different and distinct aspect to the Otemon proposal. Having moved the apartment block away from the street in order to gain privacy, a screening veil is added to further increase visual distance. This screen-device is then modifiable by being composed of a series of moving elements, each of which can be positioned by individual apartment residents.

The entire façade is thus rendered into a spatial and visual filter, allowing the interstitial zone between each apartment and the surrounding city to be alternatively opened or closed according to each resident's desire. It provides a conceptual zone of transition, negotiating the relation between the public outer chaos of the city and the relative inner calm of the apartment interiors.

Project 6:8   > Context and comment
Poolhouse   > Refer to *Landing/Poolhouse.*

Fig 1 Bathing hut

Fig 2 Portholes into pool

Fig 3 East elevation detail

Fig 4 Studio

Opposite:
East elevation

6:8.1 Precision

Nowhere is the care with which the Poolhouse design has been worked out more evident than in the spatial composition of the design, wherein every detail is considered, modulated and positioned. Beside the main pool room, the accompanying living quarters provides a nest of interlocking spaces: a living room, kitchen and dining areas, bedroom, bed deck, bathroom, shower, toilet, interconnecting stairway and a pair of underwater pool windows are all locked into place. Almost like a Chinese puzzle in its fiendish complexity, with stairs, half-ladders, windows and railings all artfully interwoven alongside the main spaces, the result is suprisingly logical and open in feel. This is particularly helped by a full-height glass screen linking visually through to the more expansive, barrell-vaulted main pool hall and, at the other end of the long axis, by a small raised deck facing out over an orchard.

The Poolhouse has attracted a series of metaphorical comparisons: a bathing hut, a modernist barn, a VW camper van on steroids, a jewellery casket, a static railway carriage have all been suggested. But it is less in the visual appearance and more in the spatial tactics of the design that the true character of the Poolhouse can be discerned: a Swiss watch-like degree of precision, whereby each spatial cog is perfectly positioned next to its neighbour, working in synchronicity to create a compact and accurate architectural machine.

Project 6:10
Jubilee School

Date
1999–2002

Location
Tulse Hill, London

Client
London Borough of
Lambeth

> **Context and comment**

> A school which is in fact several facilities on one site: a primary school, a junior school, a Special Educational Needs (SEN) school for profoundly deaf students, and a Sure-Start nursery and crèche.

> Positioned on a stepped site, the main two storey building accommodates infants on the lower level and juniors above. Infants can then step out directly onto the playground on the lowest part of the site, while juniors exit at either end of the structure and walk around to the upper part of the site where their own playground is placed.

> The SEN, with its highly specialised access requirements, and the Sure-Start facility are both positioned at the rear of the site, allowing the SEN in particular to be integrated or separated from the rest of the school as staff and pupils desire.

> A separately-articulated front element to the school incorporates a large assembly hall and cantilevered *porte-cochère*, with administration hidden underneath.

> Project won in competition.

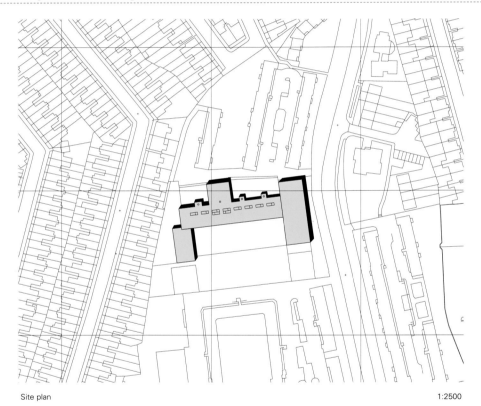

Site plan   1:2500

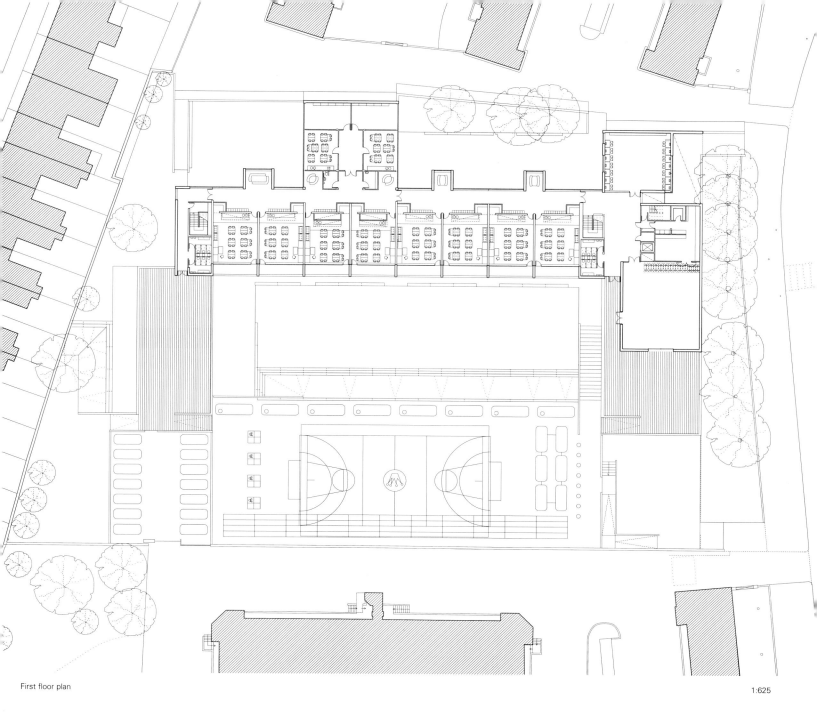

First floor plan

1:625

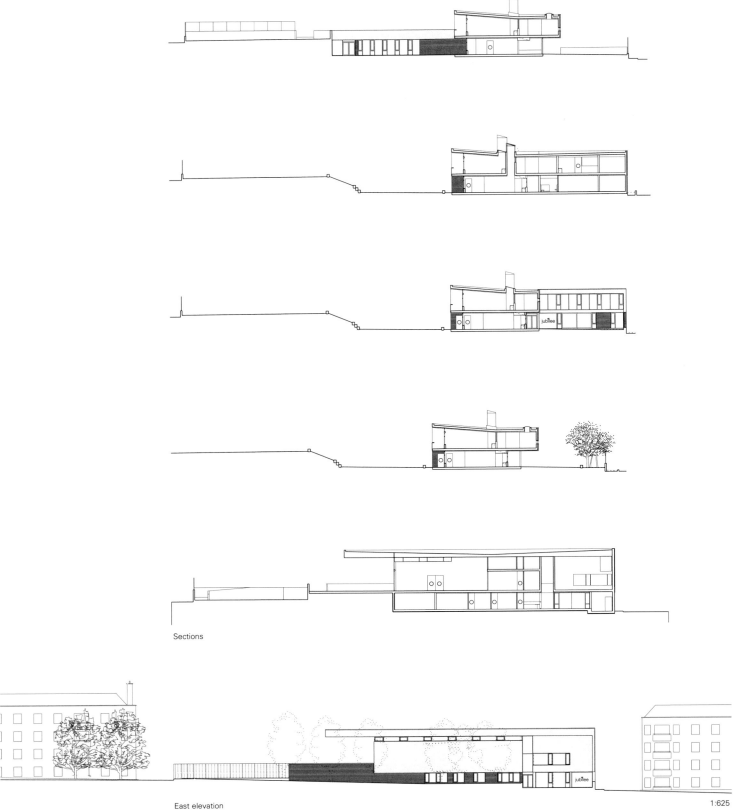

Sections

East elevation

1:625

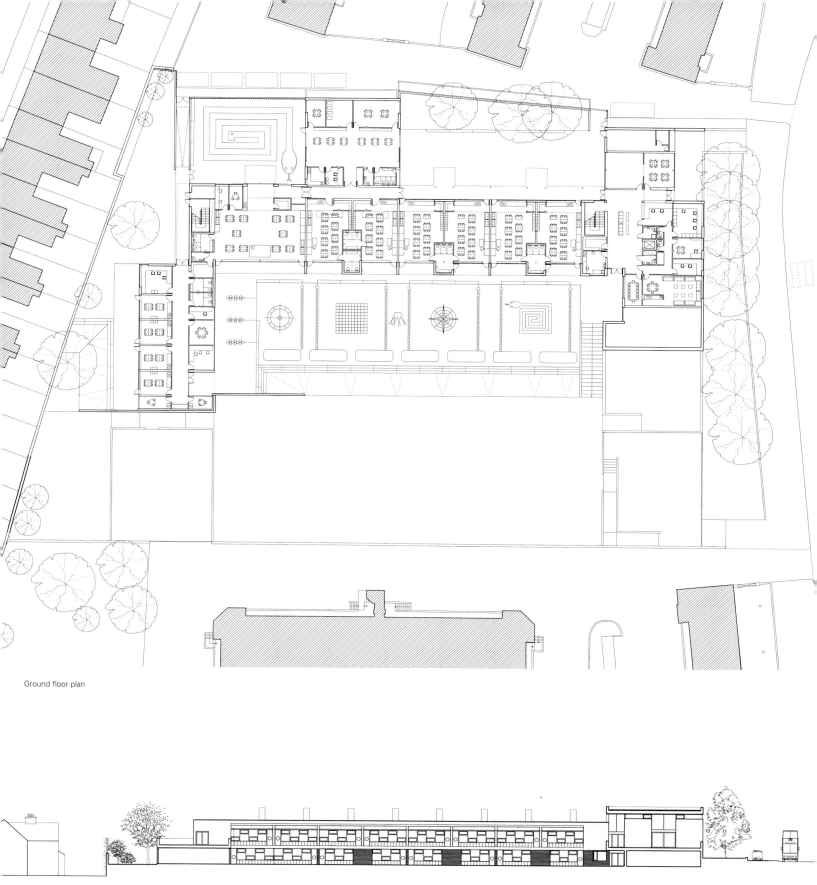

Ground floor plan

South elevation

1:625

Fig 1 Window by
       Martin Richman

Fig 2 Glazed brick plinth

Fig 3 Lighting installation
       by Martin Richman

Fig 4 Coloured cheeks

6:9.1 Ugly beautiful thing

The local community of Tulse Hill presents a robust urban context in which to situate a school for young people: gritty council estates and rough pubs face middle-class Edwardian houses and newly-built security-gated apartments, separated by a busy main road and other, less visible social barriers. Positioned squarely in the midst of this scenario, the Jubilee School presents itself confidently as a large rectilinear composition, dominated brazenly by a near blank front elevation and a massive cantilevered roof to the left.

This is not meant to be a subtle insertion, but carries a tough and almost brutalist demeanour: the cantilever does not taper, but remains resolutely thick and deep; glazed bricks at the lower lever help repel graffiti; large cheek walls guide visitors while dissuading unwanted guests from getting too close.

But it is a carefully considered and delightful insertion in many other ways: that deep cantilever is asymmetrically placed onto the school below, creating an unexpected yet welcome structural complication visible to the inquisitive eye; those hard glazed bricks shimmer in the late afternoon lights as parents arrive to collect their children; the cheek walls are painted in purples and pinks, and, once navigated, lead visitors into an elegant entrance area complete with pink-lit glazed reception desk.

It is an ugly beautiful thing, this school, not afraid to be either urban or architectural, strong enough to be both commanding and aesthetic.

6:9.2 Modulations

Move further into the project, and the overall disposition of the project into its separate schools, each with its own zones for teaching and playing, becomes immediately clear. Such a necessarily rigorous spatial disposition could, however, have led all too easily into a rigid production-line-like atmosphere. Yet this has been carefully avoided by a sprinkling through out the school of many different tactics of disruption and surprise.

Toilets – so essential to the physical and psychological well-being of children – are precisely located and sized according to the ages of those concerned, and get the kind of long mirrors, stainless steel washbasins, painted walls and glazed lighting that would be more usually seen in trendy West End bars than in state schools. The artist Martin Richman, working closely with the office, has dispersed a blizzard of coloured wall and lighting elements around the school, creating a subtly-fracturing and modulation of the more rigid architectonic nature of the plan. Studio Myerscough have similarly added graphics to playground surfaces, while light-and-wind chimneys provide unexpected penetrations of nature into the building interior.

The result is a balance of order and disorder, plan and movement, certainty and surprise, architecture-as-material and architecture-as-experience.

Fig 5 IT room

Fig 6 Break-out space

Fig 7 Furniture designed
for the school by
Andrew Stafford

Fig 8 Playground seen
from SEN roof

Fig 9 School entrance

6:9.3 Corners

One of the key characteristics of the project is
the way in which dominant spaces – classrooms,
corridors, assembly hall – easily and frequently give
way to subsidiary areas. For example, break-out
spaces for the junior school classrooms sit in adjacent
cantilevered boxes, a nature study area is positioned
right to the edge of the site, while the SEN school
can assume either complete separation or tentative
connectivity with the rest of the project through the
opening of doors and use shared play areas. Children
love being in public, but they also love their own
private corners, and the Jubilee School project is
happy to provide both.

6:9.4 Development

While the final plan arrangement looks effortless,
it is actually a process of complex refinement and
negotiation. In particular, great chunks of consultation
period were needed to get all of the separate schools
to talk to each other, while two judicial reviews on the
planning process further complicated matters at key
stages of design progression.

A series of plan and compositional proposals
facilitated the various stages of this developmental
process, and the thoroughness of the spatial
investigations involved.

Fig 11 Coloured cheeks,
      glazed bricks

Fig 12 The cantilevered roof of
      the hall creates an area
      for outdoor assembly

Fig 13 Sedum-covered roof with
      light-and-wind chimneys

Fig 14 Classroom elevation

Opposite top: School hall

6:9.5 Temporality

Providing for 420 school children of various different ages and sizes is a complex affair and, apart from the different playgrounds, alternative entrances and routes through have to be incorporated. The effect is to layer distinct speeds and temporalities on to the site, ceding to the various occupants' usage patterns whenever required. These temporal and spatial layers are not entirely separated, and still allow for interaction and encounters, but without forcing their conjuncture.

In a similar manner, the outside community is also welcomed into the facility in the evenings, at weekends and other times. In particular, separating out classrooms from the main assembly hall and playgrounds allows adult and teenage access to these facilities under controlled circumstances.

Spacing the school thus means not only accommodating its spatial elements but also its temporal patterns, and weaving them together into one coherent architecture.

14

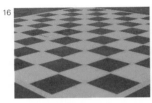

Fig 15 Cantilevered box providing
sheltered play area

Fig 16-17 Playground games

Fig 18 Cantilevered roof
to school hall

Opposite: Nursery
playground

Pages 213-214:
View across school
to Central London

Pages 215-216: View
from Tulse Hill

Going for a drink?
Even if you're not a drinker, it's a socially useful way of breaking the ice.

So much has been spoken and written in the last ten years about collaboration between artists
and architects, or other professionals, but in my view much of this misses an essential point, which
is how we are in one another's company.

If everybody is anxious and self-conscious there's unlikely to be a free flow of thought and ideas
bubbling around the arena, whereas if we respect one another's endeavours and are comfortable
with each other, the barriers break down and space is created whereby an inventive interplay can
take place. Thus the usefulness of allowing social time within a collaborative process.

So AHMM people are inveterate boozers who cannot be pulled from the pub? No, but the ones I've
worked with over the years allow space for relationships to develop and give a huge enthusiasm to
their projects which is infectious and stimulating. They become people you want to spend time with,
people who make one feel brighter, sparkier for their presences. They seem open to elements of
serendipitous discovery within the process, allowing for shifts of emphasis, whilst retaining a unifying
vision of the whole.

In the projects I have worked on with AHMM we have tended to enjoy many of our confluential
moments, and so it often feels natural for someone to ask at the end of the day, 'going for a drink?'

Martin Richman

Project chronology

Project name	Description	Client	Location	Designed	Completed
West Pier 2000	The winning entry in an ideas competition for the refurbishment of the West Pier in Brighton.	Building Design/British Steel	Brighton	1988	
417-425 Finchley Road	A development of 35 apartments for a private client.	Michael Scott	West Hampstead, London	1989	
Porsche Showroom	A car showroom and service centre for Porsche.	JCT 600	Newcastle	1989	
Otemon Housing	A design competition for a block of 48 apartments for a Japanese private developer.	TED Associates	Fukuoka, Japan	1990	
Fifth Column	A rooftop studio extension for a T-shirt printing company.	Fifth Column	Kentish Town, London	1990	
Poolhouse	An indoor swimming pool and guesthouse. RIBA Award 1996	David & Beryl Allford	Wiltshire	1990	1994
Sunny Gardens Road	A loft conversion for a private client.	John Alexander	Hendon	1990	
Rotherwick Road	The refurbishment of a listed Parker and Unwin house within Hampstead Garden Suburb.	G Ostacchini/Peters	Hampstead Garden Suburb, London	1990	1991
Clitterhouse Café	The conversion of a roadside cafe.	Margaret McGovern	Cricklewood, London	1990	1990
323 Finchley Road	Obtaining a restaurant licence.	Mr Has	West Hampstead, London	1990	
Longhouse	A family house for a private client.	Richard Dewey	Wiltshire	1990	1996
Watt-Thorn House	A residential conversion incorporating a sound recording studio.	Ben Watt and Tracey Thorn	Hampstead, London	1990	1990
American Embassy Exhibition Space	A visitor's reception and exhibition area.	United States Government	US Embassy, Grosvenor Square, London	1990	
Paternoster Alternative	A series of theoretical propositions for this City development site culminating in an exhibition.		The Architecture Foundation, St James, London	1990	1990
Melvin Apartment	The refurbishment of a top floor apartment.	Jeremy Melvin	Waterloo, London	1991	1992
Mitchell House	The refurbushment of a terraced house.	Patrick Mitchell	Vauxhall, London	1991	1992
Halas Archive	A studio and archive store for a film animator.	John Halas	Hampstead, London	1992	1994
Triton Square Proposals	The re-ordering and remodelling of Triton Square within the Euston Centre complex.	The British Land Company Plc	Euston, London	1992	
9 Gough Square	The extension and refurbishment of barristers' chambers.	Lingwood Estates	Holborn, London	1992	1994
RIBA Under £50 K	An exhibition of architects' projects with a construction value below £50,000.	Royal Institute of British Architects	Gallery Two, RIBA, London	1992	1992
Yokarutu Apartment Building	A feasibility study for prototypical student housing.	TED Associates	Japan	1993	
Brent Reading Recovery	A teaching facility for children with reading difficulties.	Rose Ive	Brent, London	1993	1993
Sofer House	The refurbishment of a private house.	David Sofer	Primrose Hill, London	1993	1994
Gilbert House	The refurbishment and extension of a village house.	Colin Gilbert	Cambridge	1993	1994
Designing for Doctors	An exhibition illustrating the value of good design in the primary health sector.	British Medical Association	BMA Headquarters, London	1993	
Law Courts Competition	A competition entry with YRM for a 100,000 sq. metre law courts complex in Riyadh.	YRM	Saudi Arabia	1994	
St Giles Day Care Centre	The refurbishment and extension of a day-care centre for the mentally ill.	Maudsley and Bethlem NHS Trust	Peckham, London	1994	

Project name	Description	Client	Location	Designed	Completed
Live-in Room House	A vision of the house of the future as part of the New British Architecture exhibition.	The Architecture Foundation	St James, London	1994	1994
Myerscough House	The refurbishment of a private house.	Henry and Betty Myerscough	Holloway, London	1994	1994
Mallett-Catcheside House	The conversion of a former shop to a family house.	Lee Mallett & Kim Catcheside	Canonbury, London	1994	1996
Morris House	The conversion of a former barn into a residential annexe.	Robert and Audrey Morris	Oxfordshire	1994	1996
Wright House	The refurbishment of a Grade II listed town house.	Jonathan and Annabel Wright	Islington, London	1994	1995
Private Apartment	The fit-out of a 2000 sq. ft. apartment in a 1930s warehouse building.	David & Beryl Allford	North London	1995	1996
Skye House	The development of the Live-in Room House project for a crofter's site on Skye.	Colin MacKinnon	Isle of Skye, Scotland	1995	
Portsmouth Players	The refurbishment of an existing thatched barn and the creation of a new linked two-storey building to provide rehearsal facilities for an amateur dramatic company.	John Lindsey	Portsmouth	1995	1999
14 Burlington Arcade	A shop fit-out for a Malaysian jewellery retailer.	Royal Selingor	Piccadilly, London	1995	1995
North Croydon Medical Centre	A new GP surgery replacing an existing surgery on the site. RIBA Award 1999, Civic Trust 2001	Dr Robert J Trew	Croydon	1994	1998
St Mary's Nursery School	St Mary's Nursery School forms part of a project to refurbish and renovate the existing Junior and Infants School.	RC Diocese Westminster	Kilburn, London	1994	1996
Corn Exchange Hoarding	The winning entry in a design competition for building hoarding in the City of London.	The British Land Company Plc	City of London	1994	1995
Tottenham GP Surgery	A new GP Surgery on the ground floor of a mixed use development.	Tottenham FHSA	Tottenham, London	1994	1996
Allford Apartment	The re-configuration of two flats into a duplex apartment in Camden.	Simon Allford	Camden, London	1995	1996
Walsall Bus Station	The winning entry in an open design competition for a new bus station. RIBA Award 2001, Civic Trust Commendation.	Centro	Walsall, West Midlands	1995	2000
Talbot House	The refurbishment of a large family house in Dulwich.	John and Jenny Talbot	Dulwich, London	1995	1996
Heaton House	The refurbishment and extension of a house in the Barnbury Conservation Area	Jill Heaton	Barnsbury, London	1995	1996
Alchemy	The fit-out of a shop unit in Covent Garden for fashion retailer Alchemy.	Ruth Allford and Natalie Stratos	Covent Garden, London	1996	1996
Coolhurst Club	The development of an existing tennis club to provide new changing facilities, a gym and 3 squash courts	Coolhurst Lawn Tennis and Squash Club	Crouch End, London	1996	
Strangely Familiar	An exhibition revealing urban ideas and stories from artists, architects, theorists and writers.	Royal Institute of British Architects	Gallery One, RIBA, London	1996	1996
European Academy	The refurbishment of two neighbouring Grade 2 listed houses to create a new cultural centre.	European Academy	Belgravia, London	1996	1997

Project name	Description	Client	Location	Designed	Completed
Morelands	The refurbishment and re-configuration of a former light industrial complex into offices.	Derwent Valley Property	Clerkenwell, London	1996	1999
Cranley Place	The refurbishment and fit-out of a Grade II listed townhouse for a private client.	Steve Davis	Kensington, London	1996	1997
Latimer Park	A headquarters office building for a high-tech components retailer.	Electrocomponents	Burton Latimer, Leicstershire	1996	
Valentine Volvo	A car showroom and service centre for Volvo.	Shaun Alderman	Salford	1997	
Thorogood-Lipworth Apartment	The refurbishment of a private apartment.	Kevin Thorogood & Karen Lipworth	Swiss Cottage, London	1997	1998
Edge Hill Theatre	The winning entry in a design competition for a traditional 350-seat theatre, 150-seat studio theatre and gallery with cafe and restaurant.	Edge Hill University	Ormskirk, Lancashire	1997	
Broadgate Club West	A new health club on the ground floor of a new office development. RIBA Award 1998.	The British Land Company Plc and Broadgate Club Plc	Euston, London	1997	1998
Private House	Obtaining planning and conservation area consent for a new build house in the Highgate Conservation Area.	Private client	Kenwood, London	1997	
Our Lady of the Rosary School	A three form extension to an existing primary school.	RC Diocese Westminster	Staines, Middlesex	1997	1999
Great Notley Primary School	The winning entry in a design competition for a model school demonstrating sustainable principles within a standard DfEE budget. Civic Trust Award 2001, RIBA Award 2000, RIBA Sustainability Award, Royal Fine Arts Commission Trust Award 2000.	Essex County Council/ Design Council	Black Notley, Essex	1997	1999
IDEO Offices	An office fit-out for a product design company.	IDEO	Clerkenwell, London	1997	1999
Grays Inn Road	The refurbishment of two office buildings removing staircases and lifts to create a single building.	Pilcher Hershman	Grays Inn, London	1997	1999
CASPAR	The winning entry in a design competition to design prototypical city-centre apartments for single people at affordable rents. Egan Demonstration Project, British Construction Industry Award 2001.	Joseph Rowntree Foundation	Birmingham	1997	2000
Smith & Milton offices	Office fit-out for a brand design company.	Smith & Milton	Clerkenwell, London	1997	1998
Silver House	The refurbishment of a listed townhouse.	Simon and Rebecca Silver	Maida Vale, London	1997	1998
Allford Apartment	The refurbishment of a private apartment.	Sally Allford	Kennington, London	1997	1998
Finch House	This extension of a family house in Wandsworth.	Paul and Susannah Finch	Wandsworth, London	1997	2000
Millennium Products	A touring exhibition for the Design Council, created to celebrate the Government's 'Millennium Products' initiative.	Design Council	Various	1998	1998
Perseverance Works	A mixed-use live-work development.	London Buildings	Shoreditch, London	1998	
Dalston Lane	A development of 18 dwellings over 750 sq m of retail.	Peabody Trust	Dalston, London	1998	1999
Highgate Road Studios	A masterplan for the refurbishment of a large mixed-use development.	London Buildings	Kentish Town, London	1998	2000

Project name	Description	Client	Location	Designed	Completed
Portpool Lane	The refurbishment of a commercial property with the addition of a rooftop extension.	Pilcher Hershman	Grays Inn, London	1998	1999
Ravensbourne College LRC	Conversion of an existing building within the campus to create a new learning resource centre.	Ravensbourne College of Design and Communication	Ravensbourne, Kent	1998	1999
Monaghan House	The refurbishment of a family house.	Ian and Helen Monaghan	Queens Park, London	1998	1998
Somerset House Terrace	A design competition for a restaurant enclosure on the riverside terrace of the former offices of the Inland Revenue.	Somerset House	Embankment, London	1998	
Work & Learn Zone	A shell and core exhibition building in collaboration with WORK to contain the 'Work and Learn' exhibition for the New Millennium Experience. RIBA Award 2000.	Tim Pyne/WORK	Greenwich, London	1998	1999
Raines Dairy	A volumetric housing scheme using prefabricated construction techniques to provide 61 dwellings. Housing Forum Demonstration Project, Housing Design Award 2001.	Peabody Trust	Stoke Newington, London	1998	2003
Granada Television	The fit-out of Granada Television's London offices.	Granada TV	Waterloo, London	1999	2000
Hat & Mitre Court	The refurbishment of a commercial property.	Private client	Clerkenwell, London	1999	1999
11-29 Fashion St	The shell and core refurbishment of commercial premises.	Fashion Street Regeneration Ltd	Whitechapel, London	1999	2000
Farringdon Road	The shell and core refurbishment of commercial premises.	Pilcher Hershman	Farringdon, London	1999	2001
Union Street	A speculative office development to provide 18,000 sq ft of 'loft style' offices.	Union Street Limited	Southwark, London	1999	2001
Northburgh Street	The shell and core refurbishment of commercial premises.	East City Investments	Clerkenwell, London	1999	2000
Goswell Road	The shell and core refurbishment of commercial premises.	Derwent Valley Property	Bloomsbury, London	1999	2001
Rosen House	The refurbishment of a private house	David and Debra Rosen	Maida Vale, London	1999	2000
Regents Place Ladies Gym	The addiiton of a ladies-only gym facility to the Broadgate Club.	Holmes Place	Euston, London	1999	2000
Beecham House	The refurbishment of a family home complete with swimming pool.	Robert and Claire Beecham	Primrose Hill, London	1999	2002
St Cross Street	The shell and core refurbishment of commercial premises.	Pilcher Hershman	Hatton Garden, London	1999	2001
Jackson House	The refurbishment of a private house	David and Rosalind Jackson	Bushey, Hertfordshire	1999	2000
Top Notch Derby	The fit-out of a new gym facility.	Top Notch	Derby	1999	2000
Britannia Street	The refurbishment of an existing stables building to provide offices.	Pilcher Hershman	Kings Cross, London	1999	2002
Architectural Association	Various refurbishment works to the school's premises.	Architectural Association	Bloomsbury, London	1999	
Jubilee School	A new 420-place community primary school, nursery and 'Surestart' facility on the site of the existing Brockwell Primary School. RSA Award.	London Borough of Lambeth	Tulse Hill, London	1999	2002
Monsoon	The rehabilitation of a Grade II* listed building originally designed for use as a British Rail Maintenance Depot. Royal Fine Arts Commission Trust Award.	Monsoon Plc	Maida Vale, London	2000	2001

Project name	Description	Client	Location	Designed	Completed
Crown Street Buildings	A mixed-use retail and residential development adjacent to the Grade 1 listed Corn Exchange. Housing Design Award 2001	Welbeck Land	Leeds	2000	2003
Rock Style	An exhibition designed in collaboration with Studio Myerscough to display some of the best-known costumes in the history of pop and rock music.	Barbican Centre	Barbican, London	2000	2000
Clearwater Yard	A new build speculative development providing 11,500 sq ft of open plan office space.	Latitude Investments	Camden, London	2000	2002
Paddington Waste Depot	A masterplan for the reconfiguration of existing waste facilities beneath the Westway.	Chelsfield Plc	Paddington, London	2000	
Union Square	A mixed-use scheme comprising four new buildings and a new urban square.	Lake Estates/Dorrington Estates	Southwark, London	2000	
Thompson House	The refurbishment of a private house.	Neil and Lisa Thompson	Fulham, London	2000	2001
Spectrum House	The shell and core refurbishment of commercial premises.	Derwent Valley Property	Kentish Town, London	2000	2002
Barbican	A masterplan for the refurbishment of the grade II listed Barbican Centre's foyer spaces with the aim of improving wayfinding.	Barbican Centre	Barbican, London	2000	2005
The Farmiloes Building	The refurbishment and extension of a former warehouse building adjacent to Smithfields market.	Baylight Properties	Clerkenwell, London	2000	2004
Waterside Café	Refurbishment of the Barbican Centre's self-service restaurant.	Barbican Centre	Barbican, London	2000	2001
Allford Apartment	The reconfiguration and refurbishment of a top floor mansion flat in Marylebone.	Simon Allford	Marylebone, London	2002	2003
New Garden House	The refurbishment and extension of an office building to create approximately double the existing floor area .	Wilmar Estates	Hatton Garden, London	2001	2005
Shelter offices	The refurbishment of the charity's head office.	Shelter	Clerkenwell, London	2001	2003
Simon House	The refurbishment of a private house.	Peter Simon	Chelsea, London	2001	2002
214-222 St John Street	A feasibility study for a mixed use development where the building form has been generated by the complex 'rights of light' angles imposed by adjacent properties.	Chelsfield Plc	Clerkenwell, London	2002	
Centric House	Masterplanning for re-development of an existing complex of 1900-1930s warehouse buildings.	Derwent Valley Property	Shoreditch, London	2001	2004
Private residence, North London	A new family home located on a vacant site in North London.	Private client	North London	2001	2003
Storey's Way	The refurbishment of a Grade II listed Baillie-Scott house.	John and Jenny Talbot	Cambridge	2001	2003
Monsoon Bridge	A new pedestrian bridge crossing the canal at Little Venice.	Monsoon Plc	Maida Vale, London	2001	
MoMo Apartments	Exploring the feasibility of providing a re-locatable system of mass produced housing for families who find themselves temporarily homeless, and designed to occupy sites only temporarily available (3-10 years).	Peabody Trust	Various	2001	

Project name	Description	Client	Location	Designed	Completed
Monaghan-Pivaro Apartment	The extension and refurbishment of a top floor flat in Waterloo.	Paul Monaghan and Alicia Pivaro	Waterloo, London	2001	2002
Allen-Stock House	The refurbishment of a private house.	Isabel Allen and Jonathan Stock	Camden, London	2001	
Southwark Child Development Centre	A new facility providing both in-patient and out-patient care for children.	South East London Shared Services Partnership	Peckham, London	2001	
Wells Street	A mixed use development including 44 flats.	East City Investments	Hackney, London	2002	
Custom House Square	A masterplan for the provision of 150 new dwellings and retail units in a phased development.	Peabody Trust/LB Newham	Newham, London	2002	
New Trends in Architecture	A touring exhibition of European and Japanese architects.	Arc-en-Reve Gallery/ Hillside Forum	Japan	2002	**2002**
Cornwall Terrace	The refurbishment and conversion of a Grade I listed property to provide a marketing and conference building for British Land.	The British Land Company Plc	Regent's Park, London	2002	
Barbican Gallery Environment	A series of works to improve environmental conditions in the Barbican's main Art Gallery including filling in the existing floor void to separate the gallery from the foyers below.	Barbican Centre	Barbican, London	2002	2003
Wilson Apartment	The fit-out of a 16th floor penthouse apartment with in Goldfinger's Elephant and Castle Apartment.	Judith Wilson	Elephant & Castle, London	2002	2003
Berners Street	The refurbishment and extension of a commercial property.	Latitude Investments	Oxford Street, London	2002	
Kentish Town Health Centre	The winning entry in a design competition for a protypical health centre.	Camden NHS Primary Care Trust	Kentish Town, London	2002	
LoCo	A research project into a protoypical design for low cost offices	Research project		2002	
107 York Way	A new development of 14 flats including 4 duplex apartments.	Michael Scott	Camden, London	2002	
Gloucester Crescent	A new development of 12 apartments.	Indigo Properties	Camden, London	2002	
Barking Town Centre Masterplan	A masterplan for the extension of the existing town library together with the creation of new civic spaces in Barking Town Centre.	Urban Catalyst	Barking	2002	
Baron's Place	A feasibility study for a modular housing development.	Peabody Trust	Southwark, London	2002	

Fig 1 Alchemy

Fig 2 Our Lady of the Rosary School

Fig 3 Comp

Fig 4 Edge Hill Comp

5

6

7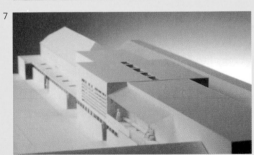

8

9

10

11

Clients for projects include:

Shaun Alderman
John Alexander
Isabel Allen and Jonathan Stock
David and Beryl Allford
Ruth Allford and Natalie Stratos
Sally Allford
Simon Allford
Arc-en-Reve Gallery/Hillside Forum
Architecture Foundation
Architectural Association

Barbican Centre
Baylight Properties
Robert and Claire Beecham
Broadgate Club Plc
British Council
Building Design/British Steel
The British Land Company Plc
British Medical Association

Camden NHS Primary Care Trust
Centro
Chelsfield Plc
Coolhurst Lawn Tennis and Squash Club

Steve Davis
Derwent Valley Holdings Plc
Design Council
Richard Dewey
Dorrington Estates

East City Investments
Edge Hill University
Electrocomponents
Essex County Council
European Academy

Farmiloes
Fashion Street Regeneration Ltd
Paul and Susannah Finch
Fifth Column

Colin Gilbert
Granada Television

John Halas
Mr Has
Jill Heaton
Holmes Place

IDEO
Indigo Properties
Rose Ive

David and Rosalind Jackson
JCT 600

Lake Estates
Latitude Investments
John Lindsey/Portsmouth Players
Lingwood Estates
London Borough of Brent
London Borough of Lambeth
London Borough of Newham
London Buildings

Margaret McGovern
Colin MacKinnon
Lee Mallet and Kim Catcheside
Maudsley and Bethlem NHS Trust
Jeremy Melvin
Patrick Mitchell
Ian and Helen Monaghan
Paul Monaghan and Alicia Pivaro
Monsoon Plc
Robert and Audrey Morris
Henry and Betty Myerscough

New Millennium Experience Company

G Ostacchini/Peters

Peabody Trust
Pilcher Hershman
Tim Pyne/WORK

Ravensbourne College of Design and Communication
David and Debra Rosen
Joseph Rowntree Foundation
Royal Institute of British Architects

Michael Scott
Royal Selingor
Shelter
Simon and Rebecca Silver
Peter Simon
David Sofer
South East London Shared Services Partnership
Somerset House
Smith & Milton

John and Jenny Talbot
TED Associates
Neil and Lisa Thompson
Kevin Thorogood and Karen Lipworth
Top Notch
Tottenham FHSA
Dr Robert J Trew

Union Street Limited
United States Government
Urban Catalyst

Ben Watt and Tracey Thorn
Welbeck Land
RC Diocese Westminster
Wilmar Estates
Judith Wilson
Jonathan and Annabel Wright

YRM

Consultants for projects include:

Adams Kara Taylor
Alsop Zogolovitch Urban Studio
Anthony Blee Consultancy
Appleyard & Trew
Arambol Associates
Arup
Atelier One
Atelier Ten
Atelier Works

B & B UK Landscape
Nelson Bakewell
Alan Baxter & Associates
BDSP
BH2
Bickerdike Allen
Black Box AV
Jinny Blom Landscape Design
David Bowden Associates
Boyden & Co
John Brady Associates
Peter Brett Associates
Sandy Brown Associates
Budgen Partnership
Buro Four

Cameron Taylor Brady
Campbell Reith Hill
Clark Smith Partnership
Jenny Coe
The Richard Coleman Consultancy
Cook & Butler
Curtins Consulting Engineers

Davis Langdon & Everest
Peter Deer & Associates
Dewhurst MacFarlane & Partners

Montagu Evans

Faber Maunsell

Gillespies
Paul Gillieron
Murdoch Green

Buro Happold
HBSV
Malcolm Hollis
Garth Hurden Associates

Jackson Coles
John Prewer Associates Ltd
Cundall Johnston & Partners
Jones Lang Wootton

Ian Keane Ltd
Tania Kovats & Alex Hartley

Max Fordham Plc
MBM Architects SA
MDA Group
Mind's Eye
Monal Associates
Studio Myerscough

Pell Frischmann
Peverley & Wheater
Pilcher Hershman
Michael Popper Associates
Price & Myers

Martin Richman
Robert Rummey Associates

FJ Samuely and Partners
Sir Frederick Snow & Partners Ltd
Andrew Stafford
Cyril Sweet Ltd

Techniker

Walker Management
Watkins:Dally
Jane Wernick Associates Ltd
Whitby Bird
Elliott Wood Partnership

Contractors for projects include:

Aiver Contracts Ltd
Allenbuild Turner
Atro Contractors Ltd

Ballast
Beck Interiors

Carlton Beck
Carty Building Contractors
Chorus Group Ltd
Courtney Builders
Donal Coyle and Sons
Cummings & Atkinson Ltd

WH Davis
Durkan Pudelek Ltd

Fiske Interiors
F R Dewey & Sons

Interior plc

Jackson Building
Jarvis Construction

Kvaerner Trollope & Colls

MBC Construction Ltd

Redcon Building Contractors
Rooff Ltd
Rydon Construction Ltd

EC Sames
Shepherd Construction
Sindall Construction Ltd
John Sisk & Son Ltd

Tolent Construction
JR Tickner

Wallis
Wates

Yorkon

Partner Biographies

Simon Allford
Simon Allford was born in London in 1961. He was educated at the University of Sheffield and then at the Bartlett School of Architecture. Previously at Nicholas Grimshaw and Partners and then at BDP, he co-founded Allford Hall Monaghan Morris in 1989.

Simon is a lecturer at the Bartlett School of Architecture where together with Paul Monaghan he has run a unit since 1989. He has also taught at Nottingham University and is a regular visiting critic and/or external examiner at a number of schools, most notably the Architectural Association; Liverpool University; the Mackintosh School of Architecture; the Kent Institute of Art & Design and the Welsh School of Architecture.

Simon is Honorary Secretary and Treasurer of the Architectural Association and is an advisor to the RIBA on Competitions/Education Policy and Strategy. He has chaired and judged a number of international competitions for the RIBA and other bodies and is involved in an advisory capacity for a number of organizations including the Construction Industry; the Steel Construction Institute; M4I (Movement for Innovation); the Architecture Club; and Architectural Research Quarterly.

Jonathan Hall
Jonathan Hall was born in Montreal in 1960. He was educated at the University of Bristol and then at the Bartlett School of Architecture from where he also gained an MSc in the History of Modern Architecture. He has a further MSc in Construction Law & Arbitration from King's College London. Previously at Douglas Paskin and Partners, he also joined BDP before co-founding Allford Hall Monaghan Morris in 1989.

Jonathan is an external examiner at the University of Central England and the Bartlett School of Architecture. As well as being a contributor to various professional journals he has lectured widely on the work of the practice.

Paul Monaghan
Paul Monaghan was born in Liverpool in 1962. He was educated at the University of Sheffield and then at the Bartlett School of Architecture. Previously with YRM, Paul too worked for BDP before co-founding Allford Hall Monaghan Morris in 1989.

Paul is a lecturer at the Bartlett School of Architecture where together with Simon Allford he has run a unit since 1989. He has also taught at Nottingham University and is a regular visiting critic and lecturer at schools of architecture throughout the UK, as well as an external examiner at the University of Westminster and Southbank University

Paul represents CABE as an Enabler advising local authorities on educational projects and has chaired and judged a number of international competitions and award schemes for the RIBA and other professional bodies. Paul is a Member of the RIBA Constructive Change Committee.

Peter Morris
Peter Morris was born in Bramhall, Cheshire in 1962. He was educated at the University of Bristol and then at the Bartlett School of Architecture. Previously at Whicheloe Macfarlane, he joined his partners at BDP before co-founding Allford Hall Monaghan Morris in 1989.

Previously a design tutor at the Bartlett School of Architecture, Peter has lectured on the work of the practice at a variety of schools of architecture and other professional organisations.

Contributors

Patrick Bellew
Patrick Bellew is a Director of Atelier Ten, consulting environmental engineers.

Peter Cook
Peter Cook is Professor of Architecture at the Bartlett School of Architecture, UCL, and co-founder of Archigram.

Jon Corpe
Jon Corpe is an architect, and formerly an architecture tutor at the Bartlett School of Architecture, UCL, during the 1980s.

David Dunster
David Dunster is Roscoe Professor of Architecture at the University of Liverpool, and formerly an architecture tutor at the Bartlett School of Architecture, UCL, during the 1980s and 1990s.

Paul Finch
Paul Finch is Publishing Director of Emap Construct, and Deputy Chairman of the Commission for Architecture and the Built Environment (CABE).

Lee Mallett
Former Editor of *Building Design*, Lee Mallett is a Director of Transformer Properties.

Jeremy Melvin
Jeremy Melvin is an architectural critic, historian and educator based in London.

Farshid Moussavi
Farshid Moussavi studied at Harvard University, the Bartlett School of Architecture, UCL, and Dundee University. With Alejandro Zaera-Polo, she established Foreign Office Architects in 1992.

Cedric Price
Cedric Price studied at Cambridge University and the Architectural Association. He established Cedric Price Architects in 1960.

Tim Pyne
Architect, exhibition designer and former Director of WORK, Tim Pyne is the promoter of the M-house.

Martin Richman
Formerly a lighting designer in the music industry and theatre, Martin Richman began his full time career as an artist in 1985.

Neil Spiller
Architect and critic, Neil Spiller is Reader in Architecture and Digital Theory at the Bartlett School of Architecture, UCL.

Matthew Wells
Matthew Wells is a Partner in Techniker, Consulting Structural Engineers.

Bibliography:
General

Allford Hall Monaghan Morris: Projects 1985-89,
(London: private publication, 1989).
Simon Allford, 'This Was Tomorrow',
Housing Design Awards, (2002).
Simon Allford, 'The Measurement of Space,
Time and Architecture', *7000 Words on Housing*,
(London: RIBA, 2002), pp. 2-5.
Architecture Foundation, *New British Architecture*,
(London: Architecture Foundation, 1994).
'Business Development: Creating a Graphic Identity',
RIBA Journal, (June 1999), p. 85.
Peter Cook and Neil Spiller (eds.),
The Power of Contemporary Architecture,
(London: Academy Editions, 1999).
Liz Farrelly, 'Making More of Less',
Blueprint, (22 April 1994), pp. 22-5.
Paul Finch, 'Survival of the Fittest', *The Architects'
Journal*, (5 March 1998), pp. 35-42.
Penny Guest, 'The Architect', *Building*,
(30 August 1987), pp. 44-5.
Demetrios Matheou, 'The Fab Four on Song',
The Architects' Journal, (4 April 1996), pp. 20-1.
Jeremy Melvin, *Young British Architects*,
(Basel: Birkhäuser, 2000), pp. 7—21.
RIBA, *New Work, Future Visions: British Architecture*,
(London : RIBA Architecture Centre, 1997).
Kenneth Powell, 'The Best of British',
Perspectives on Architecture, (February-March 1996),
pp. 42-3 and 45.
'Practice: Economy and Ability', *The Architects'
Journal*, (13 December 1989). p. 70.
Kester Rattenbury, 'Bound to be Biased',
Building Design, (30 June), pp. 18-19.
Kester Rattenbury, 'Surefire Recipe for Success',
Building Design, (16 February 1996).
Ruth Slavid, 'Bright and Beautiful?',
Steel Design, (Spring 2000), pp. 9-12.
Neil Spiller, 'Allford Hall Monaghan Morris',
10x10, (London: Phaidon, 2000), pp. 32-5.
Neil Spiller (ed.), *Lost Architectures*,
(Chichester: Wiley-Academy, 2001).

Bibliography:
Individual Projects

Barbican Centre
Rowan Moore, 'Yes, It's Awful – But I Like It',
Evening Standard, (17 October 2000), p. 37.
Richard Morrison, 'Tusa Steers: The Barbican Centre',
The Times, Arts section, (16 October 2000), pp. 20-1.
Bill Rashleigh, 'Caruso St John and AHMM Rejig
Barbican', *Building Design*, (20 October 2000), p. 2.
'Listing of Barbican Leaves Architect Unfazed', *The
Architects' Journal*, (13 September 2001) p. 16.
Robin Stringer, 'Making the Arts More Accessible',
Evening Standard, (16 October 2000), p. 19.

Birmingham Good Design
Allford Hall Monaghan Morris: Projects 1985-89,
(London: private publication, 1989), pp. 10-21.
'Birmingham Quartet', *Building Design*,
(17 March 1989), pp. 26-9.
'Fab Four Hit the Right Note', *The Architects' Journal*,
(8 March 1989), p. 10.

Broadgate Club West
Robert Bevan, 'Slimming Down the Fat Cats',
Building Design, (2 May 1997), p. 8.
'A Blueprint for Health Clubs', *The Architects'
Journal*, (5 March 1998), pp. 27-34. (Texts: Isabel
Allen,
Paul Monaghan and Nick Vaughan.
Photographs: Richard Bryant/Arcaid).
Penny McGuire, 'Fit for the Blues', *The Architectural
Review*, v.204 n.1218 (August 1998), p. 79.
(Photographs: Richard Bryant/Arcaid).

CASPAR
Kahmal Ahmed and Vanessa Thorpe, 'Official Boost
for Prince's Village: Poundbury Praised in Assault
on Brookside Style of Architecture', *The Observer*,
(14 May 2000), p. 4.
Gus Alexander, 'A Step Up', *Building*, (25 February
2000), pp. 36-41. (Photographs: Paul Rhatigan).
Chris Bazlington, 'Singles Minded: Richard Best,
Director of the Joseph Rowntree Foundation",
Building Homes, (August 2000), pp. 26-8.
'British Construction Industry Awards 2001',
The Architects' Journal, special supplement,
(25 October 2001).
David Dunster, 'Caspar 1: Allford Hall Monaghan
Morris in Birmingham', *Architecture Today*, no.107
(April 2000), pp. 22-8.
'Housing Award Victory', *Building Design*,
(6 July 2001), p. 4.
Jeremy Melvin, *Young British Architects*,
(Basel: Birkhäuser, 2000), p. 21.
Josephine Smit, 'Young Brums Go For It!',
Building Homes, (November 1999), p. 10.
(Photographs: Ronen Numa).
'Upward and Mobile', special supplement
to the *RIBA Journal*, (undated, ca. 1999).
Austin Williams, 'Movement for Innovation:
Rethinking Construction', *The Architects' Journal*,
(11 May 2000), pp. 34-43.

Clearwater Yard
Amanda Baillieu, 'Rare Bloom', *RIBA Journal*,
(August 2002), pp. 28-33.

Crown Street Buildings
Kieran Long, 'A New Look for Leeds', *Building
Design*, (16 February 2001), pp. 2 and 10-11.

Corn Exchange Hoarding
'A Building Site for Sore Eyes', *Design Week*,
(7 April 1995), p. 56.
Amanda Baillieu, 'Seeing the City from a Different
Angle', *The Independent*, (29 March 1995), p. 25.
(Photograph: Glynn Griffiths).
'The Corn Exchange Hoarding Competition',
Design Week, (16 December 1994), pp. 10-11.
Liz Farrelly, 'Image Miners', *Blueprint*,
(July-August 1995), pp. 28-9.
Paul Finch, 'Art Injection for City Streetscape',
The Architects' Journal, (6 April 1995), pp. 8-9.
(Photographs: John Frederick Anderson).
Lesley Gillilan, 'Illusions of Grandeur', *The Guardian*,
'Space' supplement, (9 October 1998), pp. 6-8.

Dalston Lane
Paul Finch, 'Survival of the Fittest',
The Architects' Journal, (5 March 1998), p. 41.
Samantha Hardingham, *London: a Guide to Recent
Architecture*, (London: Ellipsis, 2001), pp. 8.22-8.23.
Jeremy Melvin, *Young British Architects*,
(Basel: Birkhäuser, 2000), p. 20.
Arian Mostaedi, 'Dalston Lane Housing Project:
Peabody Trust', *New Apartment Buildings*,
(Barcelona: Instituto Monsa de Ediciones, 2001),
pp. 184-93. (Photos: Tim Soar).
Catherine Slessor, 'Urban Geometry',
The Architectural Review, (November 1999),
pp. 58-60. (Photographs: Tim Soar).

Designing for Doctors
Designing for Doctors, exhibition pamphlet,
(undated/1993).
Paul Monaghan, 'Surgical Spirit', *Building Design*,
(19 November 1993), pp. 12-14.
Hugh Pearman, 'Sleek Practice', *The Sunday Times*,
Style & Travel section, (1 May 1994), p. 29.

Doctors' Surgery, Stamford Hill
Hugh Pearman, 'Practice Makes Perfect',
FX, (September 1996), pp. 26-30.
Jessica Cargill Thomson, 'Just What the Doctor
Ordered', *Building*, (16 August 1996), pp. 34-7.

The Fifth Man
Allford Hall Monaghan Morris: Projects 1985-89,
(London: private publication, 1989), pp. 4-5.
The Architect/Journal of the RIBA, (August 1986).

Finch House
'AJ Small Projects 2002', *The Architects' Journal*
(17 January 2002), p. 26.

Granada Television
Deborah Singmaster, 'A Change of Programme
for Granada', *The Architects' Journal*, (22 February
2001), pp. 43-8. (Photographs: Tim Soar). Reprinted
in *The Architects' Journal: Interiors Review*, n.6
(2002), pp. 3-8.

Great Notley Primary School
'AHMM Wins Creative Contest for
Sustainable School', *The Architects' Journal*,
(19 June 1997), p. 20.
Isabel Allen, 'Three Point Turn', *The Architects'
Journal*, v.210 n.17 (4 November 1999), pp. 28-37.
(Photographs: Tim Soar).
Better Public Buildings: a Proud Legacy, (London: HM
Government, 2000), pp. 6-7. (Photographs: Tim Soar).
Alastair Blyth, 'Learning through Design', *The Architects'
Journal*, (4 November 1999), pp. 44-5.
Alastair Blyth, 'Sustainability for Kids', *Building
Services Journal*, (September 1999), pp. 18-20.
(Photographs: Daniel Thistlethwaite).
Alastair Blyth and Gordon Powell,
'Sustaining Consultation', *The Architects'
Journal*, (1 April 1999), pp. 41-3.
'Climbing the Rungs: a Strategy for the Future',
*Towards Sustainability: a Strategy for the
Construction Industry*, (London, Sustainable
Construction Focus Group Report, 2000), p. 3.
Brian Edwards, 'Sustainability: Today's Agenda for
Tomorrow', *The Architects' Journal*, (6 July 2000), pp. 41-3.
Paul Finch, "Survival of the Fittest,' *The Architects'
Journal*, (5 March 1998), p. 40.
Hattie Hartman, 'Building Alliance: Behind Some
of the Most Innovative Uses of Sustainable Design
Lies a Collaboration with Atelier Ten,' *Building
Design*, (29 September 2000), pp. 23-5.
Sutherland Lyall, 'Specifier's Choice: Great Notley
Primary School,' *AJ Focus*, (December 1999),
pp. 47-8. (Photographs: Tim Soar).
Simon McEnnis, 'Eco-Friendly School Rated
Top Design For Millennium,' *Braintree Times*,
(15 June 2000), p. 3.
Simon McEnnis, 'Masterpiece: School of Future
is Building of the Year,' *Evening Gazette*, (14 June
2000), p. 1.
Simon McEnnis, 'Pioneering School that
Left the Dome Standing,' *Evening Gazette*,
(16 June 2000), p. 22.
Jeremy Melvin, *Young British Architects*,
(Basel: Birkhäuser, 2000), pp. 18-19.
Jay Merrick, 'The School in a Class of its Own',
The Independent, Arts section.
Malcolm Reading, 'Learning About Sustainability',
The Architects' Journal, (16 October 1997), pp. 48-9.
'RIBA Journal Sustainability Award 2000',
RIBA Journal, (July 2000).
Ruth Slavid, 'Keener to be Greener', *The Architects'
Journal*, (23 July 1998), pp. 46-7.
Ruth Slavid, 'What is Sustainability?', *The Architects'
Journal*, (5 February 1998), p. 44.
David Taylor, 'Essex Snubs AHMM over
Great Notley Extension', *The Architects'
Journal*, (4 April 2002), p. 5.
David Taylor, 'Prized – and Event the Users
Like Them', *The Independent on Sunday*,
(18 June 2000), pp. 18-19.
Matt Weaver, 'RIBA Rewards Sustainability',
Building Design, (16 June 2000), p. 2.

Great Sutton Street/Studio Myerscough
'Everything But the Kitchen Sink', *The Observer*,
Magazine section, (26 November 2000), p.90.
(Photographs: Gavin Kingcome).

Halas Archive
Deborah Singmaster, 'Perspective: Garage
Conversion Achieves Aethetic Effect at Low Cost',
The Architects' Journal, (27 July 1994), pp. 16-17.
(Photographs: Morley von Sternberg).

Jubilee School
Kenneth Powell, *New London Architecture*,
(London: Merrell, 2001).

Kempston Brick Monument
Jeremy Melvin, 'Monument for the Nineties',
Building Design, (30 September 1994), p. 16-17.

Live-In Room House
Christopher Lloyd, 'Bold Visions of How
the World Will Look in 50 Years' Time',
The Sunday Times, Innovation and Technology
section, (5 March 1995), p. 5.
Lee Mallett, 'A Vision of the Future House',
Estates Times, (15 April 1994), p. 12.
Clare Melhuish, 'New British Architecture:
Qualified Enthusiasm', *Building Design*,
(1994), p. 2.
Robert Maxwell, 'Show House', *RIBA Journal*,
(April 1994), p. 28.
Hugh Pearman, 'I Have a Little Plan', *The Sunday
Times*, Style & Travel section, (24 April 1994), p. 28.
Hugh Pearman, 'The Shape of Things to Come',
The Times.
Deyan Sudjic, 'Designed to Distraction',
The Guardian, (5 April 1994).
Giles Worsley, 'Home Draws', *Financial Times*.

Mallett-Catcheside House
Sarah Gaventa. 'Talking Shop', *The Sunday Times*,
Style section, (8 September 1996), pp. 26-8.
(Photographs Wayne Vincent and Geoff Beeckman).
Lee Mallett and Jeremy Melvin, 'How the Other Half
Lives', *Building Design*, (12 July 1996), pp. 16-17.
(Photographs: Geoff Beeckman).
Jeremy Melvin, 'Allford Hall Monaghan Morris',
Building Design, (12 July 1996), pp. 18-19.
(Photographs: Geoff Beeckman).

Marsham Street Alternative
'Marsham Street Revisited', *Building Design*,
(7 August 1992), pp. 12-14.

Melvin Apartment
Building Design, (30 October 1992), p. 16.
(Photographs: Dennis Gilbert).
Terence Conran, *The Essential House Book*,
(London: Conran Octopus, 1994), p. 63.
'The Hall Guy', *Evening Standard*, (London),
Homes and Property supplement.
Lucas Hollweg, 'A Word About the Home Office',
The Independent on Sunday, The Sunday Review
section, (1 December 1996), pp. 80-2.
'Office Platform', *Elle Decoration*, (March 1995), p. 96.
Lucia van der Post, 'Good Design Can Save
Money and Time', *Financial Times*, (8-9 May 1993).
Kenneth Powell (ed.), *London*,
(London: Academy Editions, 1993).

Millennium Pavilion (RIBAJ)
'British Standards', *RIBA Journal*,
(August 1996), pp. 24-7.

Millennium Products
Pamela Buxton, 'Global Product Placement', *Building
Design*, (29 January 1999), pp. 12-13. (Photographs:
Richard Learoyd).
'Competition Wins for AHMM and Timpson Manley',
The Architects' Journal, (11 June 1998) p. 9.
'Let's All Meet in the Year 2000',
Blueprint, (December 1998), p. 13.

Monsoon
'AHMM at Paddington', *The Architects' Journal*,
(8 June 2000), p. 12.
Andrew Anthony, 'Paint the Town', *Vogue*,
(February 2000), pp. 160-5.
'New Revamp for Sixties Landmark', *Building Design*,
(16 June 2000), p. 5.

Morelands
Paul Finch, 'Survival of the Fittest', *The Architects'
Journal*, (5 March 1998), p. 42.
Jeremy Melvin, *Young British Architects*,
(Basel: Birkhäuser, 2000), p. 21.
'Morelands Buildings', *The Architects' Journal*,
(5 March 1998), p. 42.
Morelands, Derwent Valley
promotional brochure, (1999).

Museum of Scotland (competition entry)
John Welsh, 'Berth of a Nation:
Museum of Scotland', *Building Design*,
(14 June 1991), pp. 30-7.

North Croydon Medical Centre
'Come the Revolution', *Building Design*,
(10 March 2000), p. 8.
Paul Finch, 'Survival of the Fittest',
The Architects' Journal, (5 March 1998), p. 41.
Lee Mallett, 'Doctoring the Planning Rules',
Building Design, (29 September 1995), pp. 18-19.
Jeremy Melvin, *Young British Architects*,
(Basel: Birkhäuser, 2000), p. 15.
John Welsh, 'In Good Shape', *RIBA Journal*,
(May 1999), pp. 36-43. (Photographs: Tim Soar).

Otemon Housing
Robert Maxwell, 'Show House',
RIBA Journal, (April 1994), p. 28.
Jeremy Melvin, 'Gridblocked', *Building Design*,
(29 March 1991), pp. 20-1.

Our Lady of the Rosary School
Paul Finch, 'Survival of the Fittest',
The Architects' Journal, (5 March 1998), p. 40.

Passport to Plumstead
Kester Rattenbury, 'Visions for Woolwich',
Building Design, (25 February 1994), pp. 15-18.

Peabody Trust Housing, Newington Green
'Green Issues', *RIBA Journal*,
(November 1996), pp. 14-19.
Josephine Smit and Jeremy Gates,
'2000: a Year in Peview', *Building Homes*,
no.1 (January 2000), pp. 12-20.

Poolhouse
Terence Conran and Michael Hall, 'Radical Designs Rise From the Lands', *Country Life*, (30 April 1998), pp. 70-2. (Photographs: Dennis Gilbert).
'Detail: A Poolhouse in Pewsey', *Architecture Today*, n.27 (April 1992), pp. 76-7.
Estelle Doughty, 'Aqua Felice: Pool-Haus bei London', *Leonardo*, (May 1994), pp. 30-1. (Photographs: Dennis Gilbert).
RIBA, New Work, Future visions: British architecture, (London : RIBA Architecture Centre, 1997).
Louise Rogers, 'Two Piece', *RIBA Journal*, v.101 n.8 (August 1994), pp. 24-31. (Photographs: Dennis Gilbert).
Giles Worsley, 'A Home of Your Own', *Perspectives on Architecture*, (March 1995), p. 35.

Portsmouth Players
Robert Bevan, 'Behind the Scenes', *Building Design*, (29 October 1999), pp. 21-2. (Photographs: Tim Soar).

Private Apartment
Isabel Allen, 'A Loft for an Entertaining Lifestyle', *The Architects' Journal*, (26 September 1996), p. 44.

Raines Dairy
Isabel Allen, 'Industry Chiefs Call for Fresh Approach to Urban Planning', *The Architects' Journal*, (1 June 2000), p. 14.
'Factory-Build: the Sequel', *Building Homes*, (January 2000), p. 16.
Housing Design Awards, *Home: A Place to Live*, (Birmingham: Housing Design Awards, 2001).
Kieran Long, 'Peabody Builds on Modular Pioneer Work', *Building Design*, (10 December 1999), p. 5.
'Modular Housing, North London', *Building*, (2 June 2000), p. 12.

Ravensbourne College
Amanda Birch, 'Bright Ideas', *Building Design*, (23 June 2000), pp. 19-21. (Photographs: Tim Soar).

RIBA Lecture
Allford Hall Monaghan Morris lecture (13 February 1996), RIBA Audio Collection A, RIBA Library, London.
Kester Rattenbury, 'Surefire Recipe for Success', *Building Design*, n.1252 (16 February 1996).

St. Mary's Nursery School
'Learning from Experience', *The Architects' Journal*, (4 April 1996), pp. 27-35. (Texts: Susan Dawson, Miriam Green, Jonathan Hall, Louis Hellman and Robert Roodhouse. Photographs: Dennis Gilbert).
Demetrios Matheou, 'Bending the Rules', *Design*, (Winter 1996), pp. 48-55.

Strangely Familiar
Iain Borden, Jane Rendell, Joe Kerr and Alicia Pivaro (eds.), *Strangely Familiar: Narratives of Architecture in the City*, (Routledge, 1996).
Iain Borden, Jane Rendell, Joe Kerr with Alicia Pivaro (eds.), *The Unknown City: Contesting Architecture and Social Space*, (MIT Press, 2001).

Theatre and Arts Complex, Edge Hill University College
Paul Finch, 'Survival of the Fittest', *The Architects' Journal*, (5 March 1998), pp. 38-9.
'Stage Debut for London Foursome', *Building Design*, (7 February 1997) p. 1.
John Welsh, 'Stage Craft', *RIBA Journal*, (March 1997) pp. 22-3.

Unit 10
Lee Mallett, 'Housey Housey', *Building Design*, (21 June 1996), pp. 12-13
'We're Not Interested in What It Looks Like', Peter Cook (ed.), *Bartlett Book of Ideas*, (Bartlett Architecture Publications, 2000), pp. 130-3.

Under 50K
Hugh Pearman, 'Budget Wares on Competitive Display', *The Architects' Journal*, (18 November 1992), p. 43.

Walsall Bus Station
Amanda Baillieu, 'Young Architects Skip Off with Walsall Prizes', *The Architects' Journal*, (9 November 1995), p. 16.
Paul Blair, 'Unveiled: Bus Station Plans', *Walsall Observer*, (17 November 1995).
Robert Booth, 'Waging War on the Forces of Mediocrity', *The Architects' Journal*, (22 June 2000), p. 6.
Iain Borden, 'The Art of the Everyday: Walsall Bus Station', *Archis*, n.5 (2001), pp. 45-8.
Nancy Cavill et al, 'West Midlands', *Building*, (12 March 1999), pp. 40-51.
Marcus Fairs, 'Ideas Above Its Station', *Building*, (16 June 2000), pp. 36-41. (Photographs: Tim Soar).
Paul Finch, 'Transport in the Round at Walsall Bus Station', *The Architects' Journal*, (1 February 1996), pp. 24-5.
Paul Finch, 'Survival of the Fittest', *The Architects' Journal*, (5 March 1998), pp. 36-7.
'Futuristic Bus Station Plan Unveiled', *Walsall Advertiser*, (16 November 1995).
Terry Grimley, 'Look Around and Wonder', *The Birmingham Post*, (22 November 1997), p. 29.
'Interchange', *The Architects' Journal*, (18 January 2001), p. 18.
Elaine Knutt, 'Moonbase Walsall', *Building*, (17 September 1999) pp. 50-4. (Photographs: Daniel Thistlethwaite).
Jane Lewis, 'Walsall Champions New Architecture in its Town Centre', *Building Design*, (10 November 1995), p. 4.
Jeremy Melvin, *Young British Architects*, (Basel: Birkhäuser, 2000), pp. 16-17.
Peter Morris, 'Walsall Bus Station Competition', *Passenger Terminal World*, (Spring 1996), pp. 62-4.
'New Bus Station is Unveiled', *Walsall Advertiser Midweek*, (21 November 1995).
Fiona Rattray, 'Top Deck', *The Independent on Sunday*, (2 July 2000), pp. 30-1.
RIBA, *New Work, Future Visions: British Architecture*, (London : RIBA Architecture Centre, 1997).
Andy Pearson, 'Roofing Special', *Building*, (17 March 2000) pp. 52-67.
'Travelling Light', *Architectural Review*, n.6 (June 2000), pp.67-9. (Photographs: Tim Soar).
'The Waiting Game', *The Architects' Journal*, (31 May 2001), pp. 24-33 (Texts: Jeremy Melvin, Aran Chadwick, Susan Dawson. Photographs: Tim Soar).

West Pier 2000
Allford Hall Monaghan Morris: Projects 1985-89, (London: private publication, 1989), pp. 8-9.
'Astragal', *The Architects' Journal*, (9 January 2003), p. 38.
'Bound for Brisbane', *Building Design*, (25 March 1988), p. 1. (Photograph: Geoff Beeckman).
Paul Finch, 'West Pier 2000', *Building Design*, (10 July 1987), p. 10.
Hugh Pearman, 'On the Crest of a New Wave', *The Sunday Times*, (19 July 1987), p. 29.

Whose House Is It Anyway?
Lucia van der Post, 'In Praise of Home Comforts and Joy', *Financial Times*, (25-26 March 1995), p. 8.

Work & Learn Zone
Jez Abbott, 'All Work, Much Play', *The Architects' Journal*, (27 January 2000), pp. 43-4 and front cover.
Gus Alexander, 'Shock Horror: I Like the Dome', *Building*, (21 January 2000), pp. 22-5. (Photographs: Daniel Thistlethwaite).
Pamela Buxton, 'Hollow Promise', *Design Week*, (21 January 2000), pp. 19-23.
Helen Carter, 'The Dome is Alive with Smells of Childhood', *The Guardian*, (25 March 1999).
James Clark, 'Book Into the Dome's School Trip', *Daily Mail*, (25 March 1999), p. 34.
Nic Fleming, 'Behave, Or Else, This is the Dome of Learning', *The Daily Express*, (25 March 1999).
Linus Gregoriadis, 'Cabbage Smells to Infuse Dome', *The Independent*, (25 March 1999).
Mark Henderson, 'Stinkbombs Add Whiff of Nostalgia to Dome', *The Times*, (25 March 1999).
Nicole Martin, 'Dome Finds Room for the Old School', *The Daily Telegraph*, (25 March 1999), p. 6.
David Pilditch, 'The Smellenium', *The Mirror*, (25 March 1999), p. 23.

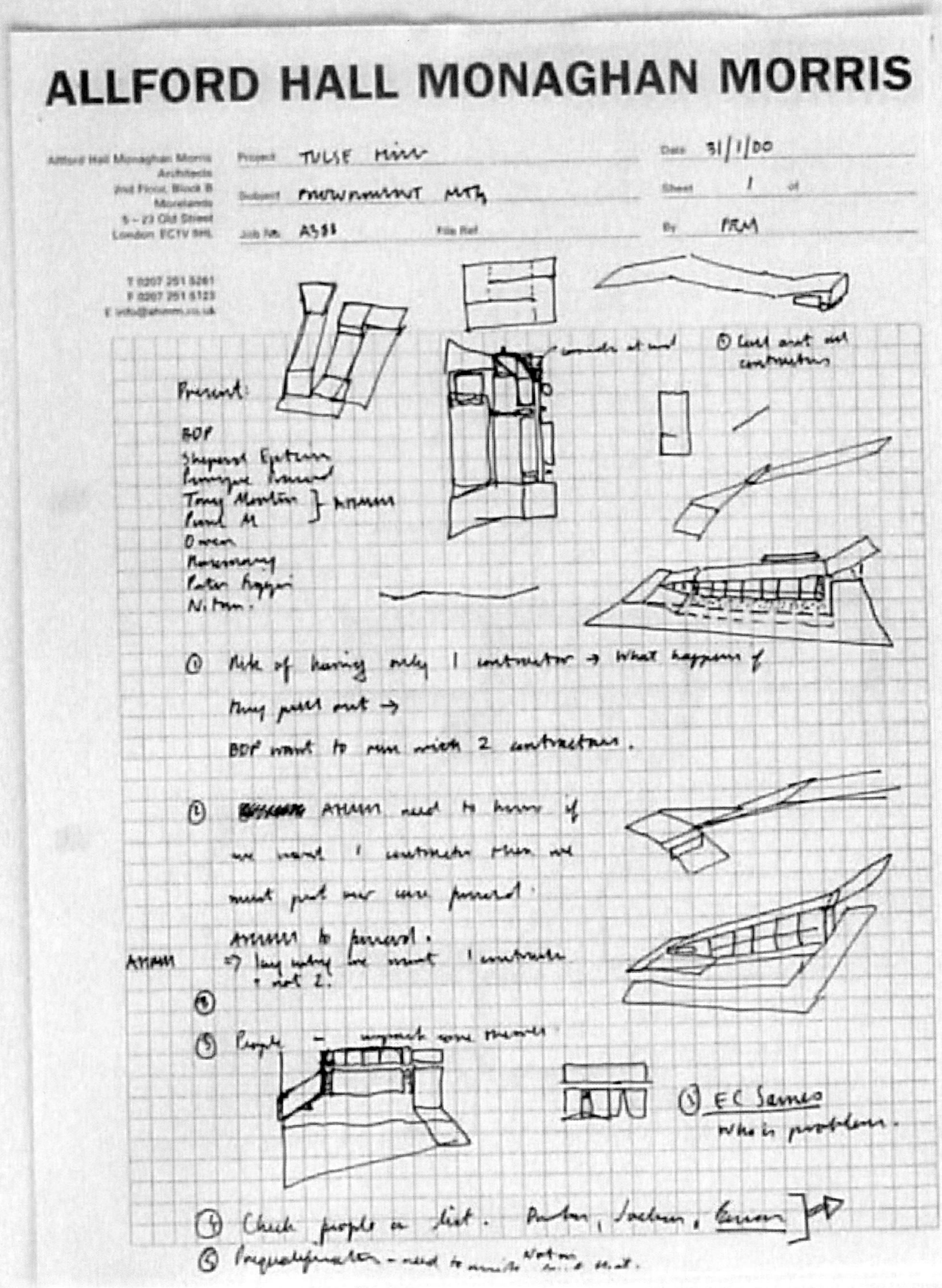

ALLFORD HALL MONAGHAN MORRIS

Allford Hall Monaghan Morris
Architects
2nd Floor, Block B
Morelands
5 – 23 Old Street
London EC1V 9HL

T 0207 251 5261
F 0207 251 6123
E info@ahmm.co.uk

Project: TULSE HILL   Date: 31/1/00

Subject: PROCUREMENT MTG   Sheet: 1 of

Job No: A351   File Ref: By: PRM

Present:

BDP
Shepard Epstein
Enrique Fraind
Tony Moulton } AHMM
Paul M
Owen
Rosemary
Peter Roger
Nitin.

① Risk of having only 1 contractor → what happens if they pull out →
BDP want to run with 2 contractors.

② AHMM need to know if we want 1 contractor then we must put our case forward.
AHMM to forward.
⇒ long why we want 1 contractor + not 2.

③

④ People — approach some others

⑤ EC James — who is problem.

⑥ Check people on list. Probst, Jackson, Carron } →

⑦ Prequalification — need to consider. Not on short list.

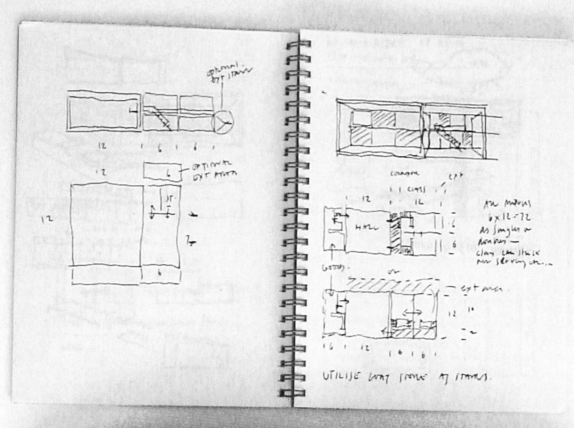

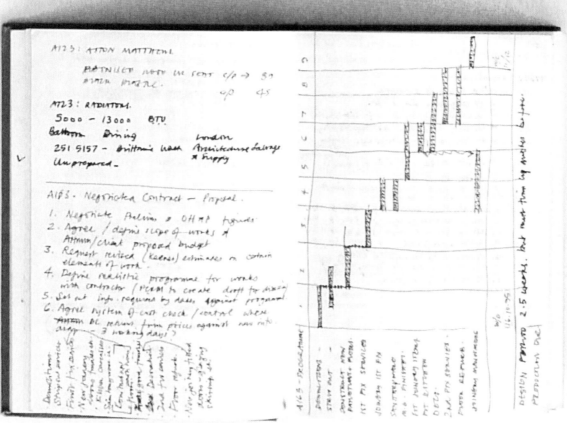

Index

Main projects included in *Manual* are in bold

Photography and image credits

Walsall Bus Station © Tim Soar 16

North Croydon Medical Centre .. ..
all © Tim Soar 20-23

CASPAR all © Tim Soar .. .. ..
except Fig.8 © Matt Chisnall 26-27

CASPAR © Tim Soar 28

CASPAR © Matt Chisnall 29

Live-In Room House © Alan Crockford .. 32-33

Portsmouth Players all © Tim Soar ..
except Fig.2 © John Lindsey 34-35

Portsmouth Players © Tim Soar 36-37

Walsall Bus Station all © Tim Soar ..
except Fig.5 AHMM archive and .. ..
Fig.9 © First House Photography 46-47

Walsall Bus Station AHMM archive 48-49

Walsall Bus Station © Tim Soar 50-54

Granada Television © Tim Soar 56

Work & Learn Zone plan of Dome ..
courtesy Richard Rogers Partnership .. 58

Work & Learn Zone © Niall Clutton .. 60-64

Walsall Bus Station all © Tim Soar .. 66

Walsall Bus Station CCTV images ..
courtesy Centro 67

Live-In Room House Tintin images ..
courtesy Hergé Foundation 68-69

Granada Television all .. ..
photographs © Tim Soar 71-73

Morelands all © Tim Soar 75

Dalston Lane all © Tim Soar ..
except Fig.3 photographer unknown .. 78-79

Crown Street Buildings site .. ..
photos: AHMM archive; model .. ..
photos © Putler/3DD 82

Broadgate Club West all © Richard Bryant
except Fig.4 AHMM archive.. 85-87

Big Breakfast AHMM archive 88

Paternoster Alternative .. ..
© Hulton Getty/Herbert Mason 90

Melvin Apartment all © Dennis Gilbert ..
except Fig.1 courtesy National Gallery .. 97

All images courtesy Studio Myerscough .. 98

Halas Archive all © Dennis Gilbert .. ..
except Fig.1 AHMM archive 101

St Mary's School Fig.5 AHMM archive, ..
Fig.2 © Jonathan Hall, Fig.3 © Matt Chisnall, ..
Fig.1, 4 and 6 © Dennis Gilbert 103

Millennium Products Fig.3 and 5-7 .. ..
© Gerald Gay, Fig.2 and 8, AHMM archive, ..
Fig.4 © Iain Borden 105-107

Millennium Products © Gerald Gay .. 108-109

Corn Exchange Hoarding all site photos ..
© John Frederick Anderson, all billboard ..
photos © Trevor Key 109-111

Poolhouse © Dennis Gilbert 112

Great Notley School all © Tim Soar .. 116-120

West Pier 2000 all © Paul Burnett .. 123-125

Monsoon © Tim Soar 128

Monsoon Fig.2 courtesy Brecht-Einzig Ltd, ..
Fig.3 © Tim Street-Porter 129

Monsoon © Tim Soar 130

Monsoon Fig.6-11 © Matt Chisnall, ..
Fig.12 © Tim Soar, Fig.8 © the artist 131

Union Square Fig.4 © AHMM archive .. 135

Poolhouse all © Dennis Gilbert ..
except Fig.1 AHMM archive.. .. 142-145

© Mel Yates 146

Designing for Doctors .. ..
courtesy Studio Myerscough 148

CASPAR Fig.1 © Tim Soar, ..
Fig.2 © Matt Chisnall 149

The Office all © Matt Chisnall 156

Dalston Lane Fig.2 and 4 © Tim Soar.. 168-169

Raines Dairy AHMM archive 172

Clearwater Yard Fig.1 and 2 © Tim Soar .. 176

Clearwater Yard © Matt Chisnall .. 177-178

Clearwater Yard © Tim Soar 179

Mallett/Catcheside House .. ..
all © Geoff Beeckman except ..
Fig.5 AHMM archive 181-183

Barbican Centre Fig.1 © Matt Chisnall, ..
Fig.3 © Smoothe 186-187

Private Apartment all © Dennis Gilbert .. 189

Great Notley School all © Tim Soar .. ..
except Fig.3 AHMM archive.. .. 192-193

Raines Dairy Fig.1, 4 and 6-9 AHMM archive, ..
Fig.2 © Smoothe, Fig.3 © Matt Chisnall .. 196

Otemon Housing all AHMM archive .. 201

Poolhouse Fig.1 AHMM archive, ..
Fig.2-5 © Dennis Gilbert 202

Poolhouse © Dennis Gilbert 203

Jubilee School all © Tim Soar ..
except p.213 © Matt Chisnall .. 208-216

Every effort has been made to trace copyright holders: any errors or ommissions are inadvertent, and will be corrected in subsequent editions if notification is given in writing to the publishers.